Caesura and *Jetztpunkt*

CAESURA AND *JETZTPUNKT*

Verse Essays after Walter Benjamin

Christopher Norris

Parlor Press
Anderson, South Carolina
www.parlorpress.com

Parlor Press LLC, Anderson, South Carolina, 29621

Library of Congress Cataloging-in-Publication Data on File

978-1-64317-510-2 (paperback)
978-1-64317-511-9 (PDF)
978-1-64317-512-6 (ePub)

1 2 3 4 5

Cover design by David Blakesley.
Cover art: "Ghost of a Genius" by Paul Klee, 1922. Oil transfer and
    watercolour on paper laid on card, collection of the Scottish
    National Gallery. Public domain.
Printed on acid-free paper.

Parlor Press, LLC is an independent publisher of scholarly and trade titles
in print and multimedia formats. This book is available in paperback
and ebook formats from Parlor Press on the World Wide Web at
http://www.parlorpress.com or through online and brick-and-mortar
bookstores. For submission information or to find out about Parlor
Press publications, write to Parlor Press, 3015 Brackenberry Drive,
Anderson, South Carolina, 29621, or email editor@parlorpress.com.

Contents

Foreword ix

Acknowledgments xiii

Image and Text *3*

Bodies: A Double-Sonnet *4*

On Film, History and Psychoanalysis *6*

Books and Toys *13*

Caesura *23*

Don't Look Now *26*

An Image from Marx *30*

Sestina: Benjamin at Port Bou *33*

On the Discrimination of Messianisms *35*

In a Picture-Gallery *39*

Story, History, *Trauerspiel* *44*

Achilles' Shield Reconsidered *51*

State of Emergency (three villanelles) *54*

Reflecting: ads and sidewalks *57*

To the Historians: a Reckoning *63*

Poetry and Language: Two Villanelles *67*

'Pure Language,' Translation, and the Seeds of Time *69*

A Collector *75*

Happiness and Terror *79*

A Plain Man Looks at the Angel of History *80*

Unforgettable *99*

Angelus Novus *101*

Redeeming the Time: Benjamin *contra* Eliot *103*

What Price the Muse? *111*

Beyond the Pleasure-Principle *116*

Contents

The Serpent's Trail *119*

Halos and *Haeccitas* (Duns Scotus, Agamben, Benjamin) *124*

Benjamin's Kafka: Failure as Destiny *129*

Art, Aura and Politics *132*

For Asja Lacis *137*

Nunc Stans: Monad and Messiah *142*

Misery and Beauty: Parables *147*

Toys and Play *149*

On Quotation, Shock, and Aura *152*

On 'Experience' *158*

Saturnine *161*

Hashish, Aura, Revolution *163*

Culture and Eros: a catechism *167*

A Thought of Emma Goldman *171*

Page-Turner *173*

Anabasis: Port Bou *175*

About the Author 179

For the Palestinians and Cor Cochion Caerdydd

Foreword

This is a sequence of poems – or verse-essays – about the great German-Jewish writer, critic, philosopher, scholar, essayist, cultural theorist, sometime poet, and political thinker Walter Benjamin. It touches on all these aspects of his work and does so in a range of rhyming and metrical verse-forms which lend themselves, in various ways, to a context-sensitive engagement with salient themes and motifs. Some of the poems are in first-person mode with Benjamin imagined as thinking, reflecting, recalling, self-questioning, or mentally rehearsing. Others are more impersonal and detached, as from the standpoint of a Benjamin reader or, if you like, the present author. One has a 'plain-man' persona confess his bafflement at how many nuances and far-reaching implications the commentators have managed to find in – or foist onto – Klee's talismanic *Angelus Novus*. A few are in dialogue form, marked or unmarked, suggesting his frequent states of chronic self-division between the various conflicting options – personal, intellectual, and political – that confronted him with often urgent, even (as it turned out) fatal life-choices.

I have allowed myself a few linguistic anachronisms where they seemed best suited to put across the gist, tone or nuanced intent of some given passage. Just as well to say also that the poems freely mix Benjamin's thoughts – and events from his life-history – with my own commentary which, on occasion, ventures beyond strict scholarly warrant. Each poem comes with one or more short epigraphs taken from his writings and offering, I hope, a useful point of entry. These were mostly the texts that inspired or prompted the poem in question and sometimes my verse comes at them from an angle that is distinct from – even somewhat at odds with – their manifest purport. Such hermeneutic licence is scarcely out of place with a writer of Benjamin's highly inventive or creative-critical temperament. Much of his work could aptly be described as prose-poetry in so far as its thought proceeds in and through the workings of rhetorical tropes such as metaphor, metonymy, synecdoche, allegory (broadly conceived), and other figures that operate as much on a large-scale structural as on a localised or textural level. One reason why Benjamin's writings have been of such interest to literary theorists, and especially to adepts of deconstruction, is the way they invite – and often anticipate – a critical reading maximally alert to the linguistic complications involved. I came to those texts and to writing these poems very much through my own longstanding fascination with just such matters of jointly philosophical and literary-critical interest.

It is especially difficult here, more so than with most thinkers, to separate the 'life' from the 'work' in any consistent or methodical way. Benjamin had a troubled and turbulent life, ending with his suicide on the French-Spanish border as a fugitive from Nazi-occupied France. What placed him in this dreadful predicament was a whole concatenation of previous decisions, influences, political pressures, career-crises, and intellectual alliances, along with subsequent fallings-out, which can be seen to have led up to that terminal event with all the implacable if hindsight-driven logic of a Greek tragedy. Prominent among them was the sheer originality – 'genius' seems the most fitting if nowadays unfashionable term – which marked almost every sentence he wrote and had various, chiefly negative and ultimately dire life-consequences. These included the failed submission of Benjamin's post-doctoral *Habilitätionschrift* and the way that his writings intrigued and impressed yet, during those crucial last months, provoked deep dissent from Theodor Adorno and fellow-members of the first-generation Frankfurt School of Critical Theory. His attempts to find a congenial home-base, or any safe niche in the lethal cross-winds of 1930s Europe, were almost foredoomed to leave Benjamin stranded on the lonely eminence of his unique intellectual temperament.

He was also very much torn – avowedly so – between an activist Marxism committed to revolutionary politics and a scholarly-contemplative absorption in textual exegesis, speculative metaphysics, cultural hermeneutics, and his own, distinctly heterodox version of scriptural commentary. In the former regard he was strongly if intermittently affected by his friend Bertolt Brecht's less ambiguous – or more forceful – commitment to Marxist theory, Communist politics, revolutionary praxis, didactic (anti-Aristotelian) theatre, and a conception of art and cultural criticism that firmly emphasised those values above the contemplative or scholarly life. In the latter Benjamin followed the example of his lifelong soulmate Gershom Scholem, a Jewish philologist, biblical commentator, and Talmudic-Kabbalistic exegete who exerted a continual counter-pressure to that which Brecht so outspokenly brought to bear. In a number of these poems I trace the shifting pattern of Benjamin's responses, a pattern that is overlaid by his likewise complex and always to some extent self-accusatory awareness of never quite managing – impossibly enough! – to satisfy both demands. Again, it is ancient Greek tragedy that often comes to mind when reviewing the calamitous series of events, historical-political and cultural-intellectual, that led up to Benjamin's exile and death.

He can perhaps most fittingly – or least restrictively – be seen as one of those writers whose texts make a nonsense of the received idea that there exists some categorical distinction between creative and critical writing, or literature and commentary on literature, or primary (imaginative) work and its secondary ('by definition' derivative) supplement. At this stage readers may well be saying 'received in what quarters, if you please?'. And they'll be right, what's more, since that idea has for a full half-century been subject to challenge by Jacques Derrida, Roland Barthes, Geoffrey Hartman, J. Hillis Miller, and many others from both sides of the notional fence who regard it as part and parcel of a Romantic ideology overly wedded to outmoded concepts like – to repeat – that of genius. All the same Benjamin's writing has something about it – something sadly lost, for very different reasons, on such otherwise well-placed comrades and colleagues as Brecht and Adorno – which makes it quintessentially an instance of creative criticism. At the time he was ploughing a solitary furrow and doing so when other, mainly political pressures made this a life-choice with consequences more than academic or cultural-intellectual. Indeed, he raises Barthes' once modish idea of 'the death of the author' to a level of significance that opens onto questions whose existential import goes wholly unaddressed by a coat-trailing essay like T.S. Eliot's 'Tradition and the Individual Talent'. (This contrast is taken up at greater length – along with other clearly-marked points of divergence between them – in 'Redeeming the Time: Benjamin *contra* Eliot'.)

I have tried to be faithful to Benjamin (so to speak) in my fashion, although here – as with previous collections devoted to Derrida and Adorno – I take the liberty of departing very markedly from the sorts of poetry that their subjects might have deemed well-chosen for the task in hand. As I have said, my verses are rhymed, metrical, formally structured, and discursive – even propositional – in mode whereas Benjamin, Adorno and Derrida took it that poetry in their time had something like an ethical as well as an aesthetic obligation to the post-Symbolist, post-Expressionist, or (however specified) Modernist order of priorities. Benjamin was never anything less than an acute, scholarly, immensely well read, and intellectually as well as – let me venture the word – spiritually profound examiner of his own along with other thinkers' ideas. It would do him an especially bad disservice not to strive for such standards when writing about his work. All the same the instantly recognisable yet elusive character of Benjamin's writing across a great range of genres and occasions is something that cannot be fully conveyed, let alone captured, in my own more prosodically and syntactically measured verse. The epigraphs were chosen partly to exemplify that tension and show how such disparities can be a source of enlivening creative, intellectual, and indeed – as Benjamin would surely have wished – dialectical stimulus. Their sources are given by book- or essay-title title only without Benjamin's name except in those few cases where another author's work is cited. All can readily be tracked down by a quick internet search. The aim with them has been to draw out by contrast what renders his texts so powerfully magnetic in their sense of mystery, intuitive insight, philosophical depth, and incisive intelligence somehow – remarkably – combined.

At times I thought the poems might serve not only as a series of reflections on Benjamin's work for already well-seasoned or knowledgeable readers but also, perhaps, as a way into life and work for those who knew very little about it or him. This felt most plausible when looking over some of the more biographically or historically oriented poems – like those about his relationships with Bertolt Brecht and Asja Lacis, or his conflicted allegiances to Marxism and the scholarly or contemplative life – which do a fair amount to fill out the picture. However the people I had mainly in mind were readers with some knowledge of Benjamin's texts and wishing to pursue angles of interest somewhat aslant to the prevailing approaches among current academic specialists. Poetry can be a highly revealing way of drawing out such angular perspectives if the verse-form is well-chosen and – what makes me a committed formalist – if they result often enough from rhyme-driven turns of thought or the complex, mentally dynamic interplay of metrical patterns and speech-rhythms. I hope this will offer adequate justification for what might otherwise appear a decidedly quixotic enterprise.

Swansea, Wales
May 2024

Acknowledgments

My thanks above all to Valerie, for her encouragement, patience, and sustaining interest as the project went along; also to David Blakesley of Parlor Press for his expert and wonderfully supportive role throughout this and three previous book projects. Thanks too, for various reasons, to Gary Day, Freda Edis, Torgeir Fjeld, Edward Greenwood, Rahim and Wendy Hassan, Peter Thabit Jones, Kathleen Kerr-Koch, Rebecca Lowe, Lucy Newlyn, Marjorie Perloff, Mike Quille, Christopher Ricks, and Alan Roderick.

Caesura and *Jetztpunkt*

Image and Text

In the fields with which we are concerned knowledge exists only in lightning flashes. The text is the thunder rolling long afterwards.

History breaks down in images, not into stories.

The Arcades Project

The lightning strikes just once and, having struck,
Then instantly restores the rule of night;
Nor will your skill, fine judgment, or good luck
Bring it again, that elemental sight.

The thunder rolls across the hills and skies
Yet's lost on watchers for the dazzling light
And scene transformed that, taken by surprise,
They failed – and fail each time – to view aright.

Just so, the text has rare thoughts to convey
But only when the vision's taken flight,
Too steeped in the emulsive light of day
Where once it blazed earth-wide from heaven's height.

'The moving finger writes,' Fitzgerald wrote,
'And having writ, moves on,' but erudite
Though we glossators are our texts denote
It's under a dark sign we live and write.

Yet let's not count that rolling 'afterwards'
Poor recompense for our belated plight
Since it may be that commentary affords
Our last, best answer to the Zeus slight.

Even in dim-lit, scribe-frequented fields
Of scholarship like ours it shines so bright,
The flash of insight, that the text it yields
Is dark-side lunar, gloss it as we might.

For while the future's master-text lies furled
In Zeus' grip we've truths to tell, despite
The thunder's lag, that may presage a world
Alert to signs less brash, more recondite.

Bodies: A Double-Sonnet

For all wisdom of the melancholic hearkens to the deep; it is won
from immersion in the life of creaturely things, and nothing of the
voice of revelation reaches it. Everything to do with Saturn points
into the depths of the earth.

The Origin of the German Trauerspiel

The idea kills inspiration; style fetters the idea; writing pays off style .
. . . The work is the death mask of its conception.

To great writers, finished works weigh lighter than those fragments
on which they labour their entire lives.

One-Way-Street

Too vitalist, those winsome tropes that draw
On life, breath, spirit, rather than disease,
Death, ailing bodies – just the similes
To conjure up the reader's sense of awe
At what 'the work' brings off, as if the *corps*
Vivant had some cachet in times like these,
Or any time when such attempts to please
The taste for life-affirming metaphor
Must sound a note more tuneful than the *corps*
Mourant that signifies: no time to tease
You, mortal reader, with apostrophes
To what may pass as 'life,' or 'spirit,' or
Their all-sustaining 'breath,' yet brings no more
To human lives or poems than the ease
Of soul that straining thread brought Damocles
By stretching his life-hopes an instant more.

For why conceive that finished thing, that tomb
Of past intent, that meaning-haunted space
Once thronged with live desires, as if it lent
'The work' a fresh vitality, or room
For Spring-like stirrings at its roots by grace
Of some weird power to check or circumvent
The course of nature? Why this curious bent
For necromantic tropes that so deface

With death's insignia life's transient bloom?
Those *Trauerspiel* images, for all their gloom,
Give stark remembrancers their proper place
Yet keep life's counter-force untouched, unspent.

On Film, History and Psychoanalysis

It is another nature that speaks to the camera than to the eye: 'other' above all in the sense that a space informed by human consciousness gives way to a space informed by the unconscious.

The camera introduces us to unconscious optics as does psychoanalysis to unconscious impulses.

'A Little History of Photography'

To articulate the past historically does not mean to recognize it 'the way it really was' (Ranke). It means to seize hold of a memory as it flashes up at a moment of danger. Historical materialism wishes to retain that image of the past which unexpectedly appears to man singled out by history at a moment of danger.

'Theses on the Philosophy of History'

1

No film director who can rival Freud
For telling how the other lives and speaks
Within ourselves, though it's on celluloid –
That realm of dreams wherein each viewer seeks
Fulfilment through the fabulous physiques,
Heroic deeds, and denouements devised
For their deluded bliss – it's there one sneaks
Such insights as Freud might have recognised
As showing what he'd guardedly surmised.

The camera sees what human eyes avoid,
Or see around, or practise learned techniques
For seeing just so far as sight's deployed,
In league with consciousness, to block the freaks
Thrown up by that deep otherness that leaks
Into our speech and would, in undisguised,
Un-sublimated form, elicit shrieks
From those, the wounded souls he analysed,
And scarcely do the job as advertised.

2

Think of the camera as a way to cut
Out ego's wilful censorship, or view
Direct, at moments, what's securely shut
Away by those defences that accrue
To ego's side when something punches through
And threatens to disrupt the fragile state
Of truce with which the psyche had made do
And which had even Freud negotiate
On terms those Viennese prudes might part-dictate.

So well attuned to psyche's wavelength, but
If he'd just known what movie-goers knew
Unconsciously and thought to tap the glut
Of riches to be had by viewers who
Could stand their censors down for just a few
Revealing moments, rather than translate
That knowledge into concepts, it would cue
Such cinematic insights as to rate
Among Freud's greatest *aperçus* to date.

3

He'd then have seen more clearly than he did
How those two mental agencies that vie
For psychic dominance, ego and id,
Must at the same time strive to have the eye
Provide their share of visual stimuli,
Whether to meet the need of consciousness
For ego's ambient world or else supply
Id's image-crunching drive with an excess
Of stuff that ego couldn't quite repress.

For there's no out-take editor whose bid
To please the censor, show 'good taste,' or try
For popular release could keep the lid
On those unruly details that pass by
The viewer's knowing gaze and, on the sly,
Recruit unconscious forces to transgress
Whatever blocks Sir Ego might pile high

Against their nifty shifts to second-guess
The scraps of ground he'd strive to repossess.

4

Truth shows, and speaks, in just those telltale gaps
Where waking thought declines to tread, or where
Some sudden space-time jolt creates a lapse
In its accustomed service-role: to bear
The conscious mind, the image-stream, and their
Well-synchronised progression safely back
To the home-ground they still aspire to share
Despite that filmic witness to the lack
Of any guard-rail to keep things on-track.

An endless quest, a journey without maps
Through hostile country laid with many a snare –
That's what they face who'd seek them out, those traps
For Freud-instructed *cinéastes* who dare
To meet the X-marked screenshot with a stare
That ditches culture's gaze for Hitchcock's knack
Of feeding them material fit to scare
Any Hays Office censor with a smack
Of how abruptly words and scenes change tack.

5

'Screen-memories' – a phrase so often heard
In different contexts that the shifts of scene,
Like filmic cross-cuts, tend to give each word
And their conjunction double scope to mean,
For Freudians, just those memories that screen
Off hideous or traumatic episodes
With others less disturbing, while between
Devout film-goers all the psychic roads
Run deep and dark to demon-haunted nodes.

'Unconscious optics' – take an image blurred
By psyche's toll, or drop-outs that convene
To leave some telling speech-act slightly slurred,
Then have the analyst reveal what's been

Repressed at ego's bidding or made clean
Of those distorting errors in the codes
That now may serve, for senses newly keen,
As Freud's 'royal road' whose open prospect bodes
Fresh revelations as each reel re-loads.

6

Old scholars part surmised what film might bring:
'*Studium*' and '*punctum*,' textual surrogates
That caught far in advance the kind of thing
Film-goers mean when one of them relates
Those moments in the cinematic greats
When something – visual detail, verbal slip,
Half-noticed cue, or scattered set of traits –
Jumps off the page (or screen) to swiftly flip
The reader/viewer's sense of present grip.

It's this sharp point, this sudden puncturing
Of their more settled, placid, studious states
Of readerly attention that may spring
To view at any time to put the skates
On scholar-feet by that which captivates
A rapt sensorium, lifts the censorship
Of joys unknown by *studium*'s advocates,
And casts the errant *punctum* loose to rip
Their codes apart on its transgressive trip.

7

By such abrupt awakenings may the course
Of history, that smoothly-flowing stream,
Encounter shocks, disruptions, and the force
Of those events that break the age-long dream
And tell the chronicler to let his theme
At last be this – the flashed-up sign that reads
'*Jetztpunkt*: so much of history to redeem
From the dead hand of *studium* lest it leads
The scholar back where cynicism breeds'.

They think time empty, those who would endorse
Its steady, even flow or have it seem
A homogeneous medium with its source
In some far-back triumphalist's regime
Which then gave savvy chroniclers a scheme
For taming history so that it proceeds
With crisis-points enough, but none extreme
Enough to flash them up, the words and deeds
They must ensure no later reader heeds.

8

Where better exercise such needful skills
In divination than by seeing more
To cinema than all those classic stills
Would have you see, or the well-vetted store
Of favourite clips, or what the censor saw
Fit to let through since taken to contain
No trace of those few moments in the raw,
Uncensored footage that, should they remain,
Might brush close-viewers up against the grain.

Yet they're the viewers, sharp-eyed for what spills
Across the bounds of image and Hayes-Law
Compliance, whose keen scansion best fulfills
The cry of history's victims: 'don't ignore
Those scraps just rescued from the out-take floor
Through some tired censor's failure to maintain
The kind of vigilance demanded for
Whichever latest stage in the campaign
To save the world for capital again!'.

9

It's Brecht who uses it to best effect,
That method, in his parables for stage
Where chroniclers allow him to select,
From China, ancient Rome, or latter-age
Chicago, Illinois, those pressure-gauge
Events or situations where the staid
Historians, ever anxious to assuage

Old wounds, soft-pedal all that might put paid
To re-runs of the victors' dress-parade.

Yet it's in movies that you'll best detect
Those covert signs by which the victims wage
A constant war that censors can't inspect
For lack of any means to disengage
Their own internal censor, or the rage
For order as it fires a fusillade
Of self-imposed, self-suffered victimage
At all attempts to raise the barricade
That else might fall to each nocturnal raid.

10

Think 'Guernica': how every hint of gloss
Was vetoed (house-paint only!); how the white,
Black, grey-scale shades avoided any loss
Of visceral impact by the viewer's flight
Into a range of hues fit to delight
Art-connoisseurs who'd rather have their eyes
Thus pleasured than offended with the sight
Of women killed, dead babies, smoke-filled skies,
Bulls gored, and silent heaven-rending cries.

And then think: should we count all colour dross
In painting, or its nuances too slight
For formal note – just vanities to toss
Aside where tyranny's arm is raised to smite
The innocent and poets have to write,
Or painters paint, what any artist tries
(Yet always fails) to represent despite
Intentions fixed against all compromise
With arty tastes in justice-seeking guise?

11

Put colours back – say, from the flag that stands
For some late-conquered state – and fill them in,
The greyscale spaces that Picasso's hands
So perfectly contrived to quiet the din

Of claim and counter-claim and so begin,
Like Goya, to give death a form that's stark
And comfortless yet may in future win
Some few a chance to make out, through the dark,
New signs of life in hope's rekindled spark.

For how else figure, in the shadowlands
Of war and tyranny, what latest sin
Against the human spirit most demands
That art respond to war in ways akin
To those that Freud found at the origin
Of every psychomachia, every mark
Of conflict, whether fought out deep within
The soul or waged as tyrants re-embark
On wars against some new heresiarch?

12

Yet it's in film, 'the movies,' that we see
Most vividly achieved the master-stroke
That disarmed mastery, left the unconscious free
To play its not-so-little tricks, and woke
The senses to insurgent shades that broke
The victor-censor's power to hold in place
Those ego-sanctioned rules that kept the folk
From sensing the chromatics of a space
Long void of any but their faintest trace.

I see it filmically, the strewn debris
That drives Klee's storm-tossed Angel, and the smoke
From every battle where, if fitfully,
I make out moving images that stoke
Imagination's fire, like that baroque
Conceit that has *Angelum Novum* face
'Time's dark and backward abysm' and yoke
At once, as that split instant sets the pace,
Past horrors to a glimpse of future grace.

Books and Toys

I have made my most memorable purchases on trips, as a transient.
Property and possession belong to the tactical sphere. Collectors are
people with a tactical instinct . . . . How many cities have revealed
themselves to me in the marches I undertook in the pursuit of books.

       'Unpacking My Books'

The particular style and beauty of toys of the older kind can be un-
derstood only if we realize that toys used to be a by-product of the
many handicrafts that were all subject to the rules and regulations of
the guilds.

       'The Cultural History of Toys'

Toy is hand-tool, not artwork.

       Note in Benjamin Archive

They ask me: have you read them, read all these
Much cherished books of yours? My answer: no,
Not all by any means, but then, if you'd
The good luck to acquire a perfect set

Of Sèvres porcelain, would you – to please
Some clueless guest – declare 'it's not for show
By aesthetes or collectors: it's for food
So grab a plate,' then eat and see them fret.

Of course there's always the desire to tease
Those earnest types, my scholar-friends, who'll go
Such lengthy ways around just to conclude
That they and I must owe a common debt

To some obscure source-text, or that the key's
Their having read so deeply and with so
Well-tuned an ear that surely they've construed
My every thought like Adam's alphabet.

Yes, I'm a reader, one who's most at ease
With books, texts, commentaries, the kind of slow

Close reading that betrays an attitude
To this extent most like the one we met

In those who think it their main task to squeeze
From books all that it's possible to know
Once every volume, page and word's been viewed
For fear that some fine thought will slip the net.

Yet still I say: why buy the line that he's
The horse's mouth, the guy who wants a blow-
By-blow account of all that we've accrued
By minute scrutiny, like teacher's pet,

Or thinks it wrong to cut down all those trees
That feed the paper-mills if books bestow
No higher wisdom than this doubtless shrewd
Advice: grab all the rare ones you can get!

It's the collector in me wants to seize
On just that well-worn charge and simply throw
It back at them, the ostentatious brood
Of print-consumers who find books that stay

Unread a source of guilt they can appease
Only by reading shelf-loads, row by row,
Till there's no bookish content they've not chewed
Often and hard enough to lift the threat.

Unpacking books: another pleasure I'd
Not willingly give up, although God knows
I've had my fill of house-moves, some to suit
My shifting needs or interests, but of late

More often seeking out some place to hide
From Hitler's roving axe-men, or from those
Who dog my steps at every point *en route*
Where I unpack, then soon repack each crate.

That's when the book-consumers ask me: why'd
A man like me seek solace for such woes

In books as mere possessions; as the fruit
Of whatsoever windfalls chance or fate

Might send my way when it was my chief pride,
As scholar-critic, so to read the prose
Of some few precious spirits that no brute
Effect of circumstance could abrogate

Their power to set all obstacles aside,
Such as the sundry perils that arose
From my forced exile or from books left mute
By physical destruction. Yet I wait

As keenly for those much-loved volumes spied
Amongst the straw as what they may disclose
When read again with senses more acute
For having once more seen that precious freight

Fetch up at my address. Here I'll reside
Perhaps a month or two, this place I chose
Partly in hopes it might thereby confute
My own declining life-chance estimate,

But also with the thought of how I'd slide
The crate-lids off and unconceal the rows
Of hallowed fonts and bindings. 'So astute,'
They'll say, 'so highly gifted, such a great

Diviner of text-secrets, yet belied
His genius by a childlike trait that owes
Less to communing with the Absolute
Than to the wish that he might supplicate

The gods of hazard, those he'd long defied
By doing things that kept him on his toes,
Whether one step beyond the Nazi boot
Or, like his Angel, forced to contemplate

The pile-up of catastrophes that bear
The name of "history"'. 'Childlike,' you say,

These curious ways of mine, and I can see
Just what you mean although, at times, the child

May have some valuable things to share,
Such as how toys, like books, can let us play
At other-world games maximally free
Of this-world penalties or charges filed

Against all revolutionaries who dare
To think they might just live to see the day
When wishful thought becomes reality
And so redeems the human wreckage piled

Behind them. Histories unpacked with care,
Again like books, may suddenly convey
A message written there, in the debris
Of wasted lives, as if the facts (so styled

By dogged chroniclers) should now declare
It time at last for us to buck the sway
Of all the victors throughout history
Whose glorious tale has us, the mob, reviled

The more for every increment to their
Triumphal stock. Toys figure here since they,
Pure playthings, might put us in mind that we
Once stood to objects not, as now, beguiled

By the fake gloss or fetishistic glare
Of play commodified, but by the way
Those toys, hand-crafted, yet in some degree
Communal artefacts, thus reconciled

The two dimensions split beyond repair
(Or so it seemed) by every hour that's prey
To capital's four-centuries-long spree
At our expense. Perhaps it's those exiled,

Like me, from home and language who most care
For toys of that sort, playthings that betray

No trace of yearning, like the bourgeoisie,
For times long past or workshops undefiled

By humdrum tasks to which all flesh is heir
Once set to work. Forget those Fabergé-
Bejewelled gold eggs, created just to be
The toys of Russian royalty as it whiled

Its last few years away. If toys are here
Our theme, along with books and all things fit
To unpack or collect, then think instead
Of toys as nascent hand-tools, like those fine

Examples – also Russian – that appear,
If you're in luck, with other sorts of kit
At village sales, turned up in someone's shed
And (luck again) without the ersatz shine

Acquired when some officious auctioneer
Lays hands on them and has their spell submit
To bourgeois norms. That's what collectors dread,
The art-restorer's touch that makes a shrine

Of every toy-museum where the gear
That first gives kids a feel for brace-and-bit
Construction or for needle matched to thread
Becomes aestheticized as one more sign

Of high-class taste. This bids the viewer steer
Far wide of any evidence that it,
The toy in question, might be one that fed
An engineer's or craftsman's future line

Of work, and not the artist-type's career
Spent trying to remove workaday grit
From cultivated pearls. It's what I said
About art's aura and its quick decline

Once reproduction enters its old sphere
Of privilege and copies are legit

For anyone save old-school critics wed
To old-style art and dealers apt to dine

Out every auction-night on what they'd clear
In a good day. No longer 'counterfeit,'
Those copies, as rich customers are led
To think, but reproduced where arts combine

With new technology and dealers fear
To tread while artists have no cause to quit
Since, though the great work's aura may have fled,
Still it's their role to bring out what's benign

About these replicas. For why revere
A cult of aura that, like Holy Writ,
Declares art the preserve of those well-bred,
Well-off, or well-connected who'll divine

The work's authentic essence while the rest,
Those not thus singled out, must satisfy
Themselves with copies which, as they attain
Technical near-perfection, yet augment

The aura-stock by a few words addressed
To adepts only. 'These may multiply,'
It says, 'until they fill the art-domain
With simulacra; yet, to the extent

That aura still continues to invest
The masterwork, it meets your practised eye
In such a manner as to ascertain
Both its and your good claim to represent

Not just a viewpoint but a viewpoint blessed
With all it takes for you few to descry
What must elude the many'. Once again
I think of certain toys, how far they went

To challenge the idea of art as quest
For that which, properly, should occupy

Some small class-fraction while the rest remain
In thrall, like those who'd made their dark descent

To Plato's cave and never thought to test
Its flickering light against the common sky
Of a real world where objects stand out plain
In sunlit forms. Perhaps that myth's what lent

My book and toy collecting special zest,
The sense (quite contrary to all that I
Said just a moment back) of some arcane
Or occult revelation, some event

Vouchsafed to me alone, or else expressed
Through allegories that spring to life through my
(Let's say) odd knack for such against-the-grain
Close readings. Maybe it's this native bent

For all that's slant, oblique, or second-guessed
That leaves a sense of something gone awry
Between that occult, Talmud-nurtured strain
Of textual brooding that Bert Brecht once spent

Such efforts to dispel and what, in jest,
He called my *plumpes Denken*. Then I'd try
To discipline my image-teeming brain
By thoughts, like his, that made me soon repent

The slide from a materialist regard
For plain home-truths plus thinking soundly based
In Marxist dialectic to the sort
Of reverie that had no proper role,

He said, in writers' work when times were hard
And subtle disquisitions went to waste
For lack of readers. So I'd end up caught
In a self-justifying rigmarole,

As when Klee's image catches me off-guard,
His great *Angelus Novus*, always placed

Just within view so as to bring up short
Not only the idea that I'm a prole

At heart, a long frustrated communard,
But also any hope that my old taste
For image-led *pèlerinages* of thought
Might serve, despite Brecht's teaching, to console

My growing sense of new escape-routes barred
Each day as further nations rush to paste
Their colours on the map. Maybe I bought
That monoprint because it filled a hole

Amongst the books and toys, or seemed ill-starred
Enough for my dark temperament, or faced
Up retrospectively to things I'd sought
To wipe from memory. But perhaps my goal,

Like that of the *flâneurs* who promenade
Those Paris shopping-malls that I showcased,
Had more to do with what Klee's image brought
By way of chances to reduce the toll

Of inner conflict. Take my own case: card-
Carrying Marxist *versus* one who traced
Fine textual details that would soon distort
And fade if *plumpes Denken* took control,

Or sounds of discord too distinctly jarred
On nerves fine-tuned. Klee's *Angelus* erased
One conflict-point at least, the drive to thwart
Whatever hours of reverie I stole

From Brecht's imperative, as if they marred
My activist commitment or disgraced
My project by such culpable resort
To art's old tricks with millions on the dole

And war just round the corner. What it showed,
That image, is how politics may take

Forms more oblique, less overt, more inclined
To parable or allegory than meets

The doctrinaire demand that lines be toed,
That art explicitly declare its stake
In that which looks ahead or lags behind,
As gauged in terms of triumphs and defeats

Or progress hastened *versus* progress slowed
By Brechtian lights. Don't get me wrong: I make
No bones about it; unless humankind
Soon gets the Marxist message he repeats

With undiminished passion, then the road
To peace, truth, and equality will break
Up right beneath their feet and time rewind
Till history's savage irony completes

Its counterflow. So if I've seemed to load
The Klee with implications fit to shake
The angel's fragile wings, or sought to find
In it some occult sense beyond what greets

The viewer's eye, then think how it bestowed,
As with the books and toys, a means to slake
My thirst for suchlike hybrids. They combined
Art's aura with a snub to the elites

Of art-world taste whose operative code
Allowed the labels 'genuine' or 'fake'
With no side-gallery or niche assigned
To items that the auction-listing treats

As not quite fitting any proper mode
Of art-production. Caught in aura's wake,
Klee's monoprint goes part-way to unbind
Itself from such propriety, yet cheats

The death-of-art brigade by debts still owed
To craft, technique, and formal traits opaque

Yet luminous enough to yield the kind
Of allegory that keeps the exegetes

In business. So, if aura should erode
To zero, still the Angel's double-take
On art and history may leave enshrined,
In multiples, an art to grace the streets.

Caesura

Thinking involves not only the flow of thoughts, but their arrest as well.

The true picture of the past flies by. The past can be seized only as an image which flashes up at the instant when it can be recognised and is never seen again.

'Theses on the Philosophy of History'

Enjambement brings to light the original gait, neither poetic nor prosaic . . . of poetry, the essential prose-metrics of every human discourse . . . . The *versura*, the turning-point, is an ambiguous gesture that turns in two opposed directions at once: backwards (*versus*) and forwards (*pro-versa*).

Giorgio Agamben, Idea of Prose

1

No thought that equably pursues its theme.
What flows too smoothly should not bear that name.
True thinking turbulates, a rocky stream.

The phoneme interrupts the semanteme
As prosody puts discourse off its aim;
No thought that equably pursues its theme.

Caesura and enjambement: no verse-scheme
That runs on undisturbed within its frame.
True thinking turbulates, a rocky stream.

In prose-thought, too, the flood-protection team
Would calm the flow which heightens just the same:
No thought that equably pursues its theme.

The blocks and twists go furthest to redeem
Thought's silent promise, its redemptive claim.
True thinking turbulates, a rocky stream.

Let thought's caesura disjoin theme and rheme,
Enjambement show whence that disjunction came.
No thought that equably pursues its theme;
True thinking turbulates, a rocky stream.

2

So with the past: catch instants as they fly,
Caesura-marked, yours momently to seize.
No flashpoint should the *Jetztpunkt* pass you by.

The prose of history begs we apply
Sound methods but ignores the victims' pleas;
So with the past: catch instants as they fly.

How let them go when millions more may die?
It's thought turned credal arms the killing-sprees.
No flashpoint should the *Jetztpunkt* pass you by.

Best if you bring to it a poet's eye
For turns, reversals, swift antitheses.
So with the past: catch instants as they fly.

Keep hold of facts: then if it goes awry,
That tale they're part of, blame the old trustees:
No flashpoint should the *Jetztpunkt* pass you by.

Chapter and verse alike may certify
False tales unless live woodmen fell dead trees.
So with the past: catch instants as they fly;
No flashpoint should the *Jetztpunkt* pass you by.

3

The past has its own metric to disclose,
Caesura-prone but right-hand justified:
'Not-poem' yields our best idea of prose.

From century to century it flows,
Erasing punctual marks of time and tide.
The past has its own metric to disclose.

Enjambement the historian scarcely knows:
Just use 'long century' book-ends, or elide!
'Not-poem' yields our best idea of prose.

Yet times there are when even scansion shows
Such signs of strain as they would lie to hide:
The past has its own metric to disclose.

It's what the prosy chronicler yet owes
To verse, what's found in no plain-writers' guide.
'Not-poem' yields our best idea of prose.

Mark the caesura as time undergoes
A break so past and future subdivide.
The past has its own metric to disclose;
'Not-poem' yields our best idea of prose.

Don't Look Now

Reception in a state of distraction, which is increasing noticeably in all fields of art and is symptomatic of profound changes in apperception, finds in the film its true means of exercise . . . . The public is an examiner, but an absent-minded one.

Many of the deformations and stereotypes, transformations, and catastrophes which can assail the optical world in films afflict the actual world of psychosis, hallucinations, and dreams. Thanks to the camera, therefore, the individual perceptions of the psychotic and the dreamer can be appropriated by collective perception.

'The Work of Art in the Age of
Mechanical Reproduction'

1

Best not attend too closely, parse each clip.
Let scenes pass unremarked, unanalysed.
Film's own advice: give consciousness the slip!

If you lose track at times, don't be surprised:
It's suchlike jolts that films alone can spring.
Let scenes pass unremarked, unanalysed.

They miss the point who never miss a thing.
Watch too intently and your thoughts go wide.
It's suchlike jolts that films alone can spring.

Film-censors parse yet come out goggle-eyed.
Film-buffs and *cinéastes* stick close-to-screen.
Watch too intently and your thoughts go wide.

Go softer-focus, skim-read the odd scene;
That's it, the open secret, free to view.
(Film-buffs and *cinéastes* stick close-to-screen.)

Insider-talk: just ask the camera-crew;
They're best-placed to provide the handy tip.

That's it, the open secret, free to view.
Best not attend too closely, parse each clip.

2

This may remind you of Freud's talking cure.
Where but in Hollywood its *mise-en-scène*?
Whose but his own, the screenplay signature?

Slips of the tongue, mind, or script-writer's pen,
All complicate the flow of fixed intent:
Where but in Hollywood its *mise-en-scène*?

Each parataxis shows some psychic bent.
Wake up, look out for them? Anything but!
All complicate the flow of fixed intent.

The best get through to the director's cut.
Something will say: leave well-enough alone.
Wake up, look out for them? Anything but!

The film has certain meanings of its own.
They come across despite, not through, his aim.
Something will say: leave well-enough alone.

It's secondary-process thoughts that tame
What viewers might be hard-put to endure.
They come across despite, not through, his aim.
This may remind you of Freud's talking cure.

3

They'd all have you attend, those with the clout!
Look sharp, look out, remain on the *qui vive*!
Just start day-dreaming and they'll bawl you out.

All lapses must be strictly by their leave.
Save them for popcorn, ads, or 'natural break'.
Look sharp, look out, remain on the *qui vive*!

Else it's just down-time for the odd out-take.
Time idly spent means watchful moments lost!
Save them for popcorn, ads, or 'natural break'.

Attention-deficit brings future cost;
You might skip crucial frames should interest lapse.
Time idly spent means watchful moments lost!

Let time-and-motion guys make good the gaps.
There's ways to fill and still the wandering mind.
You might skip crucial frames should interest lapse.

Yet why should *distrait* viewers lag behind?
They may know best what films are all about.
There's ways to fill and still the wandering mind.
They'd all have you attend, those with the clout!

4

Shades of the class-room – teacher's sharp command:
'Keep quiet, attend, don't be distracted, you!'.
Always some stick or carrot close to hand.

The same decree: wool-gathering just won't do!
Always some mischief with distracted kids.
'Keep quiet, attend, don't be distracted, you.'

Attention soon may switch to rival bids;
Let mental focus hold the mob at bay.
Always some mischief with distracted kids.

And so with film should your attention stray:
What psychic terrors stalk unlicensed there!
Let mental focus hold the mob at bay.

Right up on screen, displayed for all to share:
How should the censors then let down their guard?
What psychic terrors stalk unlicensed there!

Let them stay private, public screening barred.
Subversive stuff, those X-marked reels they've canned!

How should the censors then let down their guard?
Shades of the class-room – teacher's sharp command.

5

The tics, neuroses, hang-ups, morbid fears,
All take brute shape beneath the studio lights
In monstrous scenes played out at death's frontiers.

Two treatments this shared horror-show invites,
Freud's talking cure, the camera's watching brief:
All take brute shape beneath the studio lights.

Let no-one think they'll offer swift relief:
At best their ministry's a gift deferred,
Freud's talking cure, the camera's watching brief.

The motion barely glimpsed, the needful word:
What chance it comes on cue, gives psyche peace?
At best their ministry's a gift deferred.

Yet it's no trivial pun, that word 'release':
A timely film, the vigil borne of hope.
What chance it comes on cue, gives psyche peace?

Couch-talk and moving image: each has scope
To track those depth-charged instants through the years.
A timely film, the vigil borne of hope,
The tics, neuroses, hang-ups, morbid fears.

An Image from Marx

Marx says that revolutions are the locomotives of world history. But the situation may be quite different. Perhaps revolutions are not the train ride, but the human race grabbing for the emergency brake.

The Arcades Project

A historical materialist cannot do without the notion of a present which is not a transition, but in which time stands still and has come to a stop. For this notion defines the present in which he himself is writing history.

'Theses on the Philosophy of History'

1

'All that is solid melts,' so Karl Marx said,
'Melts into air.' Witness the speed
Of capitalist progress, so
Transformative its ceaseless need
That every effort go
Toward inventive ways to feed
The ever-changeable desires that led
To new means of production, which then fed
The new desires which guaranteed
That the pace never slow
Since set to satisfy the greed
Of capitalists and show
Consumers how they'd better heed
The signs, keep spending (till they're in the red).

Still hits the spot when you go back and read
Him once again, Marx in full flow
About how capital sped
It up, the process that would blow
Itself apart or shred
The contract that had bosses grow
Obscenely wealthy while that wealth decreed
That naught this locomotion should impede
And workers never learn they owe

To their own toil what's bled
Away in surplus value. So
The thing just goes ahead
And the worst-off once more bestow
Their dwindling little on that plundering breed.

I read it, and I think: the Marx I know,
The Marx whom they, the plunderers, dread
Lest he at length succeed
In having revolution spread
To just the folk whom he'd
Want well on board – how oddly wed
He sounds to all he'd have us overthrow
Since put in place by Loco-Shark & Co
To keep the working class in bed
With those who'd gladly lead
Them to give up their daily bread
And profit those thus freed
For yet more business-plans to tread
Them deeper down, those lowest of the low.

I see the logic: speed it up, the white-
Hot capitalist drive to make all new,
Transform what blocked the way
To social justice brought on through
The growing strength that they,
The working class, could use to do
What Marx's image bids: enlist the right
Of all those labouring masses and the might
Of new technology to shoo
The boss-class out, display
Their new-found muscle, and pursue
The new dawn of a day
Now glimpsed, perhaps, by those who crew
That loco as it thunders through the night.

I share the hope, the wish that time requite
Those victims, yield them now what's due
Their age-old suffering, pay
The bosses back in kind, and cue

The workers' turn to play
Their lead-role as the only true
Wealth-makers: jump aboard and hang on tight!
Yet sometimes I reflect: why not re-write
That passage, that heroic view
Of revolution – say,
By opting rather to construe
Its image, as Paul Klee
Once did, by a synchronic coup
That shrinks all history to one *Jetztzeit*.

In that split second, wings outspread but flight
Denied, his Angel's left to rue
The *paysage ruiné*
Of history piled in his rear-view
Scenario yet may,
By conjuring that scene, imbue
Its victims with the timely second sight
Whereby they see those wings now shining bright,
The whole class-system knocked askew,
And history's grey-on-grey
Suffused with revolution's hue
In future-charged array
Of all that Klee's fraught image drew
From its still-death shot of the history-blight.

Sestina: Benjamin at Port Bou

In a situation with no way out, I have no other choice but to end it. It is in a little village in the Pyrenees where nobody knows me that my life will be finished. I ask you to transmit my thoughts to my friend Adorno and to explain to him the position in which I saw myself placed. There is not enough time to write all the letters I would have liked to write.

> (reportedly Benjamin's last communication,
> a postcard dated September 25, 1940)

So here it is, my one last border-zone.
No going back but no way forward; the signs
Were always bad and worse each time I left
Some latest short-stay refuge. Clear to read,
Those lethal constellations where my life
And death lie open to the scholar's gaze.

What price my cultivation of that gaze,
That famous eye for detail, if its zone
Of reference finds no room for such real-life
Events or factual details, just for signs
That rival schools of exegetes can read
In ways to please all parties, right or left.

I bore their quarrels with me when I left,
Good comrade Brecht who begged me lift my gaze
From cryptic texts for once and try to read
Dispatches from the latest battle-zone,
And shrewd Adorno who deplored all signs
Of occult thinking in my work and life.

He had a point, let's face it: not a life
That came to much, and now with no time left
To make sense of those constellated signs,
Those scattered indices that met my gaze
Years back when first I strayed into their zone,
But only now, near death, have learned to read.

I'll leave my colleagues something more to read,
My eighteen 'Theses,' fragments from a life –
A damaged life – beyond the contact-zone
Of all but exiled souls, a message left
To dark cryptanalysts whose alien gaze
Alone might help decipher my last signs.

No symbol glows translucent in these signs.
They're allegories which he who runs may read,
Or he who turns a disaffected gaze
On all past portents of a better life
Such as might elevate whatever's left
Of mine into some all-redemptive zone.

Why take those signs for tokenings of life?
How learn to read the idioglyphs I've left?
What errant gaze might scan that trackless zone?

On the Discrimination of Messianisms

There is a secret agreement between past generations and the present one. Our coming was expected on earth. Like every generation that preceded us, we have been endowed with a weak Messianic power, a power to which the past has a claim. That claim cannot be settled cheaply. Historical materialists are aware of that.

As flowers turn toward the sun, by dint of a secret heliotropism the past strives to turn toward that sun which is rising in the sky of history. A historical materialist must be aware of this most inconspicuous of all transformations.

'Theses on the Philosophy of History'

1

God knows we've had our fill of strong messiahs.
In anxious times they pop up one-a-week.
No end to mortal hopes, fears and desires.

Let's not presume them charlatans or liars
But hear the hidden gist of what they speak.
God knows we've had our fill of strong messiahs.

It's a keen ear their prophet-talk requires,
One tuned to the lost life their listeners seek.
No end to mortal hopes, fears and desires.

Don't think it's god or devil that inspires
That high prophetic tone, that false mystique.
God knows we've had our fill of strong messiahs.

But do heed what's at stake if these suppliers
Of end-time visions thrive when times are bleak.
No end to mortal hopes, fears and desires.

For that's just when the crushed soul most aspires
To catch those prophecies, however weak.
God knows we've had our fill of strong messiahs;
No end to mortal hopes, fears and desires.

2

Lend weak messiahs alone a heedful ear.
They speak of things to come, but add 'not yet'.
Let go false hopes and leave your prospects clear.

A teaching hard, a discipline severe
For long-term hopers on a short-term bet:
'Lend weak messiahs alone a heedful ear'.

It tells them end-times may be nowhere near,
That hoping's close as they'll most likely get.
Let go false hopes and leave your prospects clear.

Then you'll let go, along with them, the fear
Of blank despair at end-time dates not met.
Lend weak messiahs alone a heedful ear.

The weak messiah's the one who makes it clear:
'No strong foretellings we might both regret'.
Let go false hopes and leave your prospects clear.

He begs you note his caution, not revere
His prophecies or deem the deadline set.
Lend weak messiahs alone a heedful ear;
Let go false hopes and leave your prospects clear.

3

Still it holds good, the secret promise made.
Unspoken, crushed, suppressed, still it rings true.
Only by victors is the trust betrayed.

Their victories trash all thought of debts unpaid.
They yield no ruined life the membrance due.
Still it holds good, the secret promise made.

Those unsung martyrdoms may yet be weighed
And all their pains redeemed in future view.
Only by victors is the trust betrayed.

No strong messiah can turn the cavalcade
Of victors as we weaker ones may do.
Still it holds good, the secret promise made.

Sometimes I half-think that's the role I've played,
A weak messiah, but good to see it through.
Only by victors is the trust betrayed,

Victors and strong messiahs whose tone conveyed
A covert kinship with the lordly crew.
Still it holds good, the secret promise made;
Only by victors is the trust betrayed.

4

Think what a switch of roles may bring about!
Some unmarked deaths gain posthumous acclaim.
No permanent demise, the victim's rout,

Nor all-time knockout blow, the victor's clout:
Justice might yet frequent the halls of fame.
Think what a switch of roles may bring about!

Yet also think: what had events turned out,
Back then, with outcomes switched from game to game?
No permanent demise, the victim's rout.

Think Spanish Civil War if you'd yet doubt
My case or question my redemptive aim:
Think what a switch of roles may bring about!

'Past triumphs stand!' – a creed the victors tout.
Past truths may yet refute them, all the same:
No permanent demise, the victim's rout.

In this at least should hopes remain devout:
That none say lastly 'no messiah came'.
Think what a switch of roles may bring about!
No permanent demise, the victim's rout.

5

Our coming was expected, long foretold,
A living bond that joins the victims dead.
No chosen few, no mighty names enrolled.

Enough that all the sufferings and age-old
Folk-memories remain our daily bread.
Our coming was expected, long foretold.

Down through the centuries those avowals hold
With griefs endured, lives sacrificed, blood shed:
No chosen few, no mighty names enrolled.

They've this in common, all the lifetimes sold,
The body-souls enslaved, the war-graves fed:
Our coming was expected, long foretold.

In memory-scraps retrieved their tales unfold,
In echoes, hints, stray mentions, things once read:
No chosen few, no mighty names enrolled,

And no God-sent Messiah in victor's mould
But the downtrodden victims in his stead.
Our coming was expected, long foretold;
No chosen few, no mighty names enrolled.

In a Picture-Gallery

The expressions of those moving about a picture gallery show ill-concealed disappointment that they only find pictures there. It is this unique existence – and nothing else – that bears the mark of the history to which the work has been subject.

One-Way Street and Other Writings

The greater the decrease in the social significance of an art form, the sharper the distinction between criticism and enjoyment by the public. The conventional is uncritically enjoyed, and the truly new is criticized with aversion.

'The Work of Art in the Age of
Mechanical Reproduction'

Only the crass inverted philistine
Will call them fools or clueless, those who dwell
Some minutes on a painting – you can tell
They love it, may have waited hours in line
To see it, look reluctant to resign
Their favoured viewing-spot – yet, come the bell,
Are doubly quick to leave, to break the spell
It cast on them, and pointedly decline
Their moment's grace. It's something in their tread,
Their almost-slouch, the way their downcast eyes
Seek out the exit-sign, that says: we've shed
An old illusion, one those artist guys
Passed off as truth but, now the magic's fled,
Leaves us poor suckers with the booby-prize.

'A fool idea,' the experts will opine:
'They're like the folk who hold a hollow shell
To one ear and can hear the ocean swell
Until taught better.' Seems those people pine
For real-world scenes instead of the cloud-nine
Projections they're so anxious to dispel
Since, being naive realists, they rebel
At any art that tends to undermine
Their grip on things. The more so when they're fed

That scenic stuff – lakes, mountains, seas and skies –
And think they have some much-loved landscape spread
Before them, only then to realise
That all along they've simply been misled
By the dab hands those experts canonise.

Too quick the critics are, I'd say, to treat
'The public' – those the art gate-keepers choose
To keep outside the gate – as folk whose views
On art, or anything, are fit to greet
With sneers at such assumed 'man-in-the-street'
Art-ignorance as led them to confuse
The codes of realist painting with a ruse
To make them think 'it's real!' and thereby cheat
The viewers of their due. For fools they'd be
Indeed if, as the mockers must suppose,
They came in hopes quite literally to see
Familiar scenes transported by who knows
What potent magic to that gallery –
How better tread on old Joe Public's toes!

I'd say the movers-round who shuffle feet
From one work to the next are viewers whose
More agile footwork simply lets them lose
More rapidly the sense of incomplete
Experience, something lost, the painter's feat
Of *vraisemblance* defeated, or – *j'accuse!* –
The artist's faithful, scene-restoring muse
Compelled by regnant tastes to take back-seat
To more 'sophisticated' tastes. No plea
So old-hat as the realist's, none that goes
So utterly against the strict decree
Of 'make it new'. Yet let us ask: should those
Who seek the exit pause, then bend a knee
To current idols as the portals close?

What disappointment greater than to find,
Till now unnoticed in your favourite
Amongst those works, the double deficit
That every work dissimulates behind

The façade of appearances designed
To keep us happy with this counterfeit
Reality while making sure to kit
Mimesis out with features to remind
Us: art, not *really* real! Why blame that 'ill-
Concealed' touch of resentment if its source
Lies not at all in some obdurate will
To crank them up, those deficits, or force
Art's inner contradictions through the mill
Where thought and senses face a sour divorce?

Klee's 'Angel,' my great talisman, a kind
Of life-long *vade mecum*, proved a fit
Companion to me when art's sacred writ
Seemed desecrated by that double-bind,
While only Klee's fraught image still assigned
To bad old times their office: to transmit
For hope's re-visioning what's left to it
Of piled catastrophe as, debris-blind,
The Angel totters back. He's seen his fill,
Been witness to the worst, and knows the course
Of future history's sure to see the kill-
Rates rise until the last of those four horse-
Men heralds of apocalypse can spill
The last few drops of blood from the last torse.

I hold it dear, that image, not through my
Desire to treat as starkly as I can
The theme 'man's inhumanity to man'
(Though that's the gravamen, I can't deny)
But more to ask myself again just why
It always seems to me, each time I scan
That cryptic voiceless scream, more powerful than
The utmost realist painters can supply
To drive the message home. Nothing to hide
Away, reserve for those art-experts keen
To show they're all clued-up and bona fide,
But nothing, either, like that landscape scene
That left the gallery-goers to decide
How self-deceived or strung along they'd been.

It makes me think: what better way than by
Klee's odd, cartoonish, childlike, near-deadpan,
Surrealist angel-face can art out-span
Those obstinate aporias that try
The limits of art-theory as of high-
Art practices and so turn what began
With cherished works becoming also-ran
Into a growing wish or need to shy
Away from suchlike stuff. Quite frankly, I'd
Concur with that – think how the silver screen
Has shaped perception so the sharpest-eyed
Response to art must alternate between
The earnest art-talk of the gallery guide
And just not knowing what her words can mean.

For don't forget: there's scarcely any sort
Of lie or subterfuge that art's not made
Its bespoke calling-card or stock-in-trade
Through odes, dynastic portraits, ploys to court
Some wealthy patron, or – as Plato taught –
The old mimetic lie that often paid
Off handsomely when used to serenade
The tyrants, rogues, and ministers who'd wrought
The worst atrocities. This might suggest
You change their tune, you art-world dwellers prone
To treat with equal scorn the doubts expressed
By those ex-lovers of mimesis grown
A-weary of its charms and those who'd test
For bugs all art that's quit its viral zone.

Think only of the Angel's pinions, caught,
Spread wide, and storm-propelled by the cascade
Of past lives, hopes, and promises betrayed
Whose precious legacy would go for naught
Unless mimetic elements still brought
Their sparse, storm-tossed materials to the aid
Of holders-out against the ambuscade
Set up each time abstraction's dull retort
Declared that image void. How re-invest
The streaming fragments with the spirit known

To their first shapers if not through the quest
For new forms of mimesis that disown,
Like Klee's, all those devised at the behest
Of tyrant, victor, critic, church, or throne?

Story, History, *Trauerspiel*

Death is the sanction of everything the story-teller can tell. He has borrowed his authority from death.

The art of story-telling is reaching its end because the epic side of truth, wisdom, is dying out.

The story-teller: he is the man who could let the wick of his life be consumed completely by the gentle flame of his story.

> 'The Story-Teller'

In each case what is quotable is not just the attitude but also the words which accompany it. These words, like gestures, must be practised, which is to say first noticed and later understood. They have their pedagogical effect first, their political effect second, and their poetic effect last of all.

> 'Brecht Commentary'

Scholarship, far from leading inexorably to a profession, may in fact preclude it. For it does not permit you to abandon it.

> 'The Life of Students'

1

'Brief candle,' says Macbeth, and only needs
The slightest breath of wind to see the flame
Die down, while – point not lost on him – the game
Of thrones or snuffings-out itself proceeds
At such a pace that now the image pleads
He view his death foretold with just the same
Stone-cold indifference as elsewhere became
The single trait that anyone who reads
A German *Trauerspiel* and duly heeds
The corpses, skulls, and patent lack of shame
Or guilt on the revenger's part may blame
For lack of 'depth' as some poor victim bleeds,
Yet thereby show how tragedy misleads
Its adepts to mistake this drama's aim.

The story-teller, too, has death to thank
For his most telling scenes and touching ends,
As well as that fine sense of how to plot
A range of fictive lives in ways that bank
On shared acceptance of how death attends
Our every deed and gives our actions what
True meaning they might have. Yet here it's not
The killer's dark soliloquy that lends
A well-told tale that fearful power to blank
All human feelings but the mortal lot
We share and which, thereby, at last transcends
The moral cesspit where those feelings sank.

2

Just look to Homer if you'd wish to see
What epic poets such as he – or they
Or, arguably, she – could do to weigh
The costs of hardship, death, contumely,
Long absence from one's true Penelope,
And suchlike woes, against the coming day
Of *nostos*, her glad welcome, and the bay
Of Ithaca regained where he whom she
So long ago waved off heartbrokenly
Now steps ashore to (let's not look away)
Put her new suitors to the sword and slay
The suitor-friendly hand-maids. Let's agree:
It's brutal stuff, alright, but who are we,
Us genocidal moderns, now to say
That we're the ones those primitives should pay
Respects to, or a moral tutor's fee?

It's worth the candle, how, despite the wick
Fast burning down and his tale swiftly brought
To guttering-point or liquefaction, still
The epic story-teller had that trick,
Or breadth of sympathy, or scope of thought,
Or ageless wisdom – call it what you will,
Though do please spare us 'transferable skill' –
To keep the story-line and structure taut
While sometimes subtly managing to prick

The bubble reputation yet fulfil
Our wish to hear how well they spoke, loved, fought,
Or tangled with the body politic.

3

All story-tellers of a certain kind,
The epic poet and those connoisseurs
Of moral chaos whose dark gift confers
On *Trauerspiel* its sombre power to find
Out haunts and charnel-houses of the mind
Where it's an ill wind that so feebly stirs
The shrouds and winding-sheets yet spurs
The masked revenger, stock role preassigned,
To follow through on plot-demands so blind
And rule-bound that, after the deed occurs,
We find our moral judgment oddly blurs,
Or feels beside the point, in such a bind
As he now faces, stoically resigned
To act out all that his baroque *auteur*'s
Lined up for him with those death-whisperers
Enlisted lest the corpse-count fall behind.

I know it wasn't temperament alone
That drew me strongly to those saturnine
And (let's agree) repellent figures whose
Sick machinations fix the moral tone
Of *Trauerspiel*, nor yet those thoughts of mine,
Set out in the book's preface, which I use
For certain speculations apt to lose
All but the keenest readers. 'Moral spine,'
What our school-teachers talked about, was shown
When they, or some of them, reviled us Jews
As lacking it, which meant: you must divine
This evil's source though it cut near the bone.

4

Three genres, three plot-outlines, and three ways
Of doing what all fictions try to do,
Make sense of things from someone's point of view,

Where 'someone's not just anyone but lays
Strong claim to be the poem's, tale's, or play's
Lead character, the man of action who,
Like Homer's brave Odysseus, made it through
Each far-flung venture, voyage, trial, or phase
Of virtue-under-siege to those last days
When *nostos* beckoned and, again in true-
Born epic-hero style, he quickly slew
The suitors and the maids, then cast his gaze
On her, the emblem of all rocks-and-stays
(Or stay-at-homes) while he's free to pursue
Whatever risk, temptation, goal, or new-
World conquest brings his feats the highest praise.

I called it 'epic wisdom,' said the lack
Of that rare quality was one that left
The modern story-teller no such wise
Capacity for knowing how to pack
The moral punch at times, though with a heft
That came of his, the teller's, native ties
With his community, not in the guise
Of some outsider's put-down, one bereft
Of that shared inwardness that makes attack
On alien grounds a senseless enterprise,
Like tracing the oft-cancelled warp and weft
Of her deft needlework when he came back.

5

Yet who's to call it 'wisdom,' that which viewed
Such conduct as self-authorised, or took
The mores honoured in some ancient book,
Given its classic status, as imbued
With values and beliefs which thus preclude
All principled objection? Just unhook
Your ethics from your lit-crit tastes and look,
I told myself, at what that attitude
Amounts to, how it gave rise to a feud
(As per the *Iliad*) whose violence shook
Two city-states, destroyed one, and forsook
The code of values they, the Greeks, had hewed

So closely to except in times when crude
Or ethnocentric interests cocked a snook
At such ideals and had us readers brook
Those epic codes, however badly skewed.

Again, how justify my curious taste
For *Trauerspiel*, that gallery of curst
Assassins, psychopaths, and villains bent
On naught but intrigue, murder, brazen-faced
Deception, and resentments quietly nursed
Until, in the Fifth Act, our malcontent
Goes full berserk and then, all passion spent,
Expires on cue? It's a grim tale rehearsed
As if to tell the tragic muse: don't waste
Our time with your time-wearied sentiment
That has great souls run up against the worst
The world can do, albeit nobly faced.

6

No question, it's a creed that must appall
The high tragedian, one that makes cruel sport
With human dignity and spares no thought
For high *sententiae* at the curtain's fall
Since solely out to mock, revile, and gall
The human spirit as it brings to naught
The tragic hero's closing self-report
And thus approximates a music-hall
Routine or brutal farce. Yet, 'all in all,'
The undeceived revenger may retort,
'It's he, that nobly-suffering guy, who's caught,
When his time's up, without the wherewithal
To make my level-headed judgement-call
And opt for a last exit of the sort
Much favoured by us true renaissance court-
Bred schemers when our prospects start to pall'.

It's 'wisdom' of a kind, a bitter fruit
Born of the culture-shift that came about
When an old feudal dispensation met
Its merchant gravediggers in ways to suit

Its melancholy mood, its growing doubt
Concerning social roles now under threat,
And, above all, a faith – unproved as yet –
That some far-distant God would see them out,
Subdue those enemies, vanquish the brute
Of nascent capital, and strike the debt
They'd once owed to the conscience-churning rout
Of values that now left them destitute.

7

Thus far my reading, Marxist-influenced
And broadly Brecht-approved, although he found
It overly abstruse in parts and bound
To alienate some, including those who sensed
In it an intellect that strained against
Their every notion of what passed as sound,
Well-marshalled scholarship. And yet, what ground
For it had they, the jobsworths who dispensed
Rough justice on my work and so commenced
A surely self-protective drive to hound
Me off their patch and put the word around
That my (to them) unreadably condensed
And wiredrawn arguments should be ring-fenced
Lest scandal dog those theses I propound
And, by contagion, they become renowned
For thoughts that leave all sober minds incensed?

And yet, truth is, my rating *Trauerspiel*
So high against the cachet long enjoyed
By tragedy – a notion they deplored,
Those mediocrities out to reveal
My fallings-short – was a ruse I deployed,
In part, as a defensive outwork shored
Against just that hostility toward
All new ideas, that striving to avoid
All thought-encounters with the kinds of real-
World pain, loss, guilt, and suffering they ignored,
Those scholar-gatekeepers who near-destroyed
My academic prospects sans appeal.

8

Still it's no vengeance-seekers' role I crave,
His brooding solitude, his deep-sworn rift
With other men except those in whose gift
It might lie to advance his plot, or save
Him from detection, or – perhaps – deprave
Some erstwhile innocent prepared to lift
Her skirts and have the destined victim shift
First into bed, then to an unmarked grave
As if by fate's decree. If I behave
And write in enigmatic ways that Swift,
That master-ironist, would soon have sniffed
Out and approved then it was him, the knave,
The hole-and-corner moralist, who gave
His death's-head imprimatur to the drift
Of my ill-starred *Habilitationsschrift*
While tragic Hieronimo stayed on to rave.

Rather my texts will haunt their every note
And query, every effort to make good,
In their own interest, on the hefty stock
Of cultural capital that went to float
Their canon of great works as understood
By – who else? – those whose task it was to mock
Those others, like myself, who took the shock
Of our modernity as best we could,
Like Baudelaire before us, yet could quote –
As witness my *Passagenwerk* – to knock
The scholar-spots off all whose livelihood
Meant countermanding every word I wrote.

Achilles' Shield Reconsidered

Mankind, which in Homer's time was an object of contemplation for the Olympian gods, is now one for itself. Its self-alienation has now reached such a degree that it can experience its own destruction as aesthetic pleasure of the first order.

To pry an object from its shell, to destroy its aura, is the mark of a perception whose 'sense of the universal equality of things' has increased to such a degree that it extracts it even from a unique object by means of reproduction . . . . The adjustment of reality to the masses and of the masses to reality is a process of unlimited scope, as much for thinking as for perception.

'The Work of Art in the Age of
Mechanical Reproduction'

What shall we see engraved now on his shield
Where poets in the martial-epic line
Have often turned reflective and revealed,
From Homer down to Auden – [*nb*: mine,
That forward-looking bit!], how what seems fine
In heat of battle lived or waged anew
In verse may warn us as they hack and hew:

'Fine, maybe, if you're off the battle-field,
Like those string-pulling gods on their cloud nine,
But best not advertised each time the yield
In fresh-spilled human blood ensures the wine-
Red seas more deeply should incarnadine
Lest some reflective memory of blue
Leave men less apt to pay the tribute due.'

Might shrewd Hephaestus not have unconcealed
The omens in that intricate design
As he close-worked the metals and annealed,
At Thetis's request, a shield to shine
With all the glory that might bring divine
Protection to Achilles, not undo
Him like dear Patroclus whom Hector slew?

But what if it's the sole defence we wield,
Our knowledge, war-engendered, that the brine
Soon tarnished epic similes and peeled
The gloss from any art that would entwine
Such scenes of peace- and wartime, or combine
Life's pleasures with the lethal derring-do
Of Homer's heroes from a gods'-eye view?

That's it: the Greeks imagined what they got
From Homer – or the sundry bards that lent
Their conjoint voices to the master-plot
Which bears that name – as if the action went
On somehow like a show where each event,
Most often bloody, happened for the sake
Of keeping drowsy, shock-proof gods awake.

Not ours, that option, or a luxury not
Now ours to take, we latecomers who've spent
(We think) these two millennia getting shot
Not only of the gods whose testament
We skim ('Bible as Lit') but of the scent
Of cruelties placidly enjoyed that make
Our hearts seem oddly undisposed to break.

Perhaps the truth is now we've come a lot
Too far along the war-path to content
Our later, battle-weary selves with what,
Back then, served to appease the god-like bent
For tranquil views of suffering that repent
No deed committed where the hero's stake
Was theirs but not its cost in new heart-ache.

And then, how think to occupy that spot
Of flawed though self-ascribed omniscient
Foreknowledge now the gods'-eye viewers blot
Their copybooks each day and each new dent
In prophet-stocks goes to disorient
Us watchers as the stage-props start to shake,
Lights dim, and every motive grows opaque.

Ask by what new contrivance we're to fill
That void of presentation, how replace
The spectacle with some less costly bill
Of mortal fare, and soon you'll have to face
This just as costly truth: that now the space
For disenchanted contemplation lies
Right there before our own war-sated eyes.

It's why the movie images now spill
Across from screen to viewer and embrace
Those epic scenes that Cecil B. Mille
Has made his trademark, scenes that would erase –
So far as possible – the remnant trace
Of looker-on detachment that denies
Our role as cheerers-on sans alibis.

Think how the Futurists now seek to thrill
Their wide-eyed followers by keeping pace
With all the latest weaponry and drill
For using it, so bringing the arms-race,
Creatively made over, all the grace
Of artefacts inventors might devise
To style mass-slaughter in aesthetic guise.

No point denouncing it, that overt will-
To-power that has its leading shock-troops brace
Themselves, their 'fans' and art-machines to kill
Whatever human residues they trace
Down stage-by-stage in the long haul from Thrace
To those self-alien subjects who comprise
The few who've yet to fully synchronise.

Extract one screen-shot, take a random still
From one of them, then ask if this, my case,
Is not borne out by every Bunker Hill
Blockbuster, every dead-eyed last grimace
Of some doomed anti-hero, or the base-
Line comeback: down and dirty, we'd advise,
Since that's the role time's extras try for size.

State of Emergency (three villanelles)

> The concept of progress must be anchored in the idea of catastrophe. That things are 'status quo' is the catastrophe. It is not an ever-present possibility but what in each case is given. Thus hell is not something that awaits us, but this life here and now.
>
> *Arcades Project*

> The tradition of the oppressed teaches us that the 'state of emergency' in which we live is not the exception but the rule. We must attain to a conception of history that is in keeping with this insight.
>
> 'Theses on the Philosophy of History'

1 (Catastrophe)

Chaos deferred: conceive no steady state!
That it hold off for now's the fallback plea.
How should the progress-storm adjust its rate?

The future odds are hard to estimate;
No instant but portends catastrophe.
Chaos deferred: conceive no steady state.

Plan as you will, catastrophe won't wait:
It's aeons back, it's now, it's yet to be.
How should the progress-storm adjust its rate?

The friends of status quo negotiate
Some way to make catastrophe shock-free.
Chaos deferred: conceive no steady state.

Re-think: catastrophe can have no date.
Why, this is it, nor are we *post-* or *pre-*.
How should the progress-storm adjust its rate?

Look backward, have catastrophe dilate
Till chaos piled sky-high is all we see.
Chaos deferred: conceive no steady state;
How should the progress-storm adjust its rate?

2 (State of Exception)

It's no exception but the victors' rule.
That's one thing they'd not have you victims know:
Emergency's the all-time victim-school.

Think it a phase, a transient state, and you'll
Fall in with Nazi jurist Schmitt and Co.
It's no exception but the victor's rule.

This state is what the fascists seek to fool
You into taking as a short-run show:
Emergency's the all-time victim-school.

Believe them, and you'll soon become the tool
Of those who'd eternise the status quo.
It's no exception but the victor's rule.

That's how it happens, how some groupuscule
Of Nazi thugs exploits the touch-and-go:
Emergency's the all-time victim-school.

Don't let the Schmitts and chaos-mongers spool
You in, have you forget t'was ever so.
It's no exception but the victor's rule;
Emergency's the all-time victim-school.

3 (Powers)

Be sure you take the point as I intend.
Catastrophe's invoked in diverse ways:
The news may reach your ears through foe or friend.

The followers of Schmitt have ears to bend.
'State of emergency' – their weasel phrase!
Be sure you take the point as I intend.

They say: 'those rights and freedoms we suspend
Will be restored once through these lawless days'.
The news may reach your ears through foe or friend.

For it's a 'brief suspension' they'll extend
Till blood and bullet mark its final phase.
Be sure you take the point as I intend.

Taken their way, 'poor fools, expect no end
To servitude' is what the creed conveys.
The news may reach your ears through foe or friend.

Our way: 'turn crisis critical and lend
This age redemptive powers – see how it plays!'.
Be sure you take the point as I intend.

Drive it your way, let victims now amend
An aeon of wrongs and see the victor pays.
The news may reach your ears through foe or friend;
Be sure you take the point as I intend.

Reflecting: ads and sidewalks

What, in the end, makes advertisements superior to criticism? Not what the moving red neon says – but the fiery pool reflecting it in the asphalt.

One-Way Street and Other Writings

For a living organism, protection against stimuli is almost a more important function than the reception of stimuli.

Baudelaire speaks of a man who plunges into the crowd as into a reservoir of electric energy. Circumscribing the experience of the shock, he calls this man 'a kaleidoscope equipped with consciousness'.

'On Some Motifs in Baudelaire'

1

Sidewalk and freeway tell what's to be told:
Reflection pure and simple, thinking-free.
The lights and shades so garish, colours bold.

Why criticise, why question what you see?
It's all there on the asphalt, in the rain:
Reflection pure and simple, thinking-free.

Then the true, unintended gist stands plain:
Forget the ads, the glitz, the bogus dreams;
It's all there on the asphalt, in the rain.

Too much the critics talk of 'is' and 'seems'.
Just take surrealism's point as read:
Forget the ads, the glitz, the bogus dreams.

They're our best clue, those ostents neon-bred.
Read Freud, then ask: what's real, what's dreaming's share?
Just take surrealism's point as read.

For you've the real *Traumdeutung* imaged there,
A lurid phantasm with truths to add.
Read Freud, then ask: what's real, what's dreaming's share?

They're held as in his magic writing-pad,
The psycho-gram of all those junk-goods sold.
A lurid phantasm with truths to add;
Sidewalk and freeway tell what's to be told.

2

They read amiss who merely criticise.
Take ads apart and still they'll haunt your sleep;
Best trust to rain-blurred images, sharp eyes!

What price high theory when you're counting sheep?
It's those pooled images then serve you best:
Take ads apart and still they'll haunt your sleep.

Why fend off that return of the repressed?
Just screen the swirligig on drowsy lids.
It's those pooled images then serve you best.

Then let the analysts put in their bids.
First off there's primary-process stuff to run:
Just screen the swirligig on drowsy lids.

The structuralists can do what's left undone;
The sidewalks show what slips that lucid gaze.
First off there's primary-process stuff to run.

No seeing through the streaked, gust-ruffled glaze:
Thought slews at its sight-ravelling interface.
The sidewalks show what slips that lucid gaze.

No billboard ad but leaves its psychic trace.
Cathexis rules! It's dreams they advertise.
Thought slews at the sight-ravelling interface;
They read amiss who merely criticise.

3

'The Viennese quack' – Nabokov's name for Freud!
No end of new tricks for the ad-man trade.
His nephew Bernays saw them well deployed.

How else explain the leading role they played,
The prompts, tags, cues, subliminal alerts?
No end of new tricks for the ad-man trade.

Viewed market-wise his ideas proved dead certs.
'We bring a plague' he said to Jung, and so –
The prompts, tags, cues, subliminal alerts.

They're what he'd soon, unwittingly, bestow,
A way of life distinctly US-style.
'We bring a plague' he said to Jung, and so

It turned out, pestilent and mercantile,
The neon red of ads in sidewalk pools,
A way of life distinctly US-style.

His message soon fired up the business schools.
'There's gold in them thar Freudian notions'; whence
The neon red of ads in sidewalk pools.

Let words and images displace, condense,
And work their spell in print or celluloid.
'There's gold in them thar Freudian notions'; whence
'The Viennese quack' – Nabokov's name for Freud.

4

Let's say it plumbed the shallows, Freud's bequest.
Let's grant, a culture conquest of a kind:
A Woody Allen film-script kind, at best.

So malleable, that new consumer mind.
'The Ego and its Own': Max Stirner lives!
Let's grant: a culture-conquest of a kind.

That Freudian stuff sells goods: it gives and gives!
Just get a wised-up shrink to join your board.
'The Ego and its Own': Max Stirner lives!

It's Freud's late 'morbid' turn they can't afford:
Massage their egos and they'll live to own.
Just get a wised-up shrink to join your board.

Sure to hit sales, the Freudian-stoic tone.
Forget all that *Jenzeits des Lustprinzips*:
Massage their egos and they'll live to own.

Enough to give your customers the creeps,
His stuff about the death-drive: best if we
Forget all that *Jenzeits des Lustprinzips*.

Then we're OK with depth-psychiatry,
We business guys – though please give it a rest,
His stuff about the death-drive: best if we
Just say it plumbed the shallows, Freud's bequest.

5

That's where surrealism does the trick.
It starts there, with the sidewalk and the ads
And pooled reflections, but declines to stick

At that and begs we analyse the fads,
The fears and fetishes they cater to.
It starts there, with the sidewalk and the ads.

'Go deeper,' it exhorts, 'this speaks to you:
Ignore those ego-boosting charlatans,
The fears and fetishes they cater to.'

Such are the surreal depths Herr Doktor scans.
He tells home-truths the ad-men would abjure:
Ignore those ego-boosting charlatans!

Not alien to him, the stuff's allure.
Think of his Hampstead house, that fetish-trove!
He tells home-truths the ad-men would abjure.

So hard the man of reason in him strove,
Yet still those atavisms hard to kick.
Think of his Hampstead house, the fetish-trove!
That's where surrealism does the trick.

6

Back to the sidewalk, rain, and neon signs.
Decoding ads will get you just so far,
Like reading critic-style 'between the lines'.

See patterns stir-crazed by each passing car:
How else conceive what's going on below?
Decoding ads will get you just so far.

Or you may look to Dali, Ernst & Co,
Take them onboard as your depth-diving guides.
How else conceive what's going on below?

It's jetsam-dodging skills their art provides,
A *Blick ins Chaos*, every system down.
Take them onboard as your depth-diving guides.

Full fathom five and lords of commerce drown.
Unwise the ad-man in his bathysphere;
A *Blick ins Chaos*, every system down.

Let Freud-plus-Dali have those shapes appear
Uncannily at home in your front room:
Unwise the ad-man in his bathysphere.

He'll wander lost through culture's catacomb
In search of cheaper, family-friendly shrines.
Uncannily at home in your front-room;
Back to the sidewalk, rain, and neon signs.

7

Just think of rain on asphalt neon-lit.
Think how the flickering glow may yet catch fire,
Incinerate the ad-man's latest hit.

Car-hire, attire, spin-dryer, deep-fryer – smart buyer!
Look down from billboard at those goods ablaze.
Think how the flickering glow may yet catch fire.

It's your unmet desires that greet your gaze.
They feed the pyre, turn up no end of trash.
Look down from billboard to those goods ablaze.

Don't fret as every dream's reduced to ash.
Knew all about desires, Nabokov's quack.
They feed the pyre, turn up no end of trash.

Always some fetish-object that you lack;
Billboard to asphalt runs Cathexis Trail.
Knew all about desires, Nabokov's quack.

A death-wish gift enclosed with every sale!
How then should we resist the ad-man's deal?
Billboard to asphalt runs Cathexis Trail.

Beyond the pleasure principle it's real,
Freud's psychic spend-now-and-pay-later bit.
How then should we resist the ad-man's deal?
Just think of rain on asphalt neon-lit.

To the Historians: a Reckoning

The tradition of the oppressed teaches us that the emergency situation
in which we live is the rule. We must arrive at a concept of history
which corresponds to this. Then it will become clear that the task be-
fore us is the introduction of a real state of emergency.

Benjamin, 'Theses on the Philosophy of History'

What matters for the dialectician is having the wind of world history
in his sails. Thinking for him means: to set the sails. It is the way
they are set that matters. Words are his sails. The way they are set
turns them into concepts.

The Arcades Project

1

It's through that debris-laden storm they tack.
How else should good historians now set sail?
No headway but requires they still look back.

Good seamanship, the dialectician's knack,
Helps dodge the rough stuff when your vessel's frail.
It's through that debris-laden storm they tack.

Swept overboard, the instruments they lack,
Long lost to history's roiling seas and gale.
No headway but requires they still look back.

As spinning compass yields to almanac,
So chronicle supplants historian's tale.
It's through that debris-laden storm they tack.

The streaming shards rip through their sails like flak,
Disrupt their narratives on every scale:
No headway but requires they still look back

And have that grim reprise take up the slack
Produced by schemes thus fore-condemned to fail.
It's through that debris-laden storm they tack;
No headway but requires they still look back.

2

No riggers' guide to how the sail's best set,
No map to plot the course or spell the means:
Dialectics now turns out the safest bet.

At least it shows the savvy how to get
One up on all those standard thought-routines.
No riggers' guide to how the sail's best set.

Then maybe they'll just scrub their mounting debt
To text-book stuff (tell that to the marines!):
Dialectics now turns out the safest bet.

Too long the dialectic made them fret,
Those method-seekers on their hill of beans:
No riggers' guide to how the sail's best set.

Plato and Kant both used it, though each let
Us know 'just till the *logos* intervenes'.
Dialectics now turns out the safest bet.

Historians, how still trust in what's, as yet,
The rule that leads to those war-ravaged scenes?
No riggers' guide to how the sail's best set;
Dialectics now turns out your safest bet.

3

A strange tradition, that of the oppressed,
One solely bent to end tradition's rule:
What else should such long servitude attest?

How now bid earth 'receive an honoured guest,'
Though Auden welcomed Yeats to public school:
A strange tradition, that of the oppressed.

For it's tradition's crises that possessed
Most power to draw the fiercest ridicule.
What else should such long servitude attest?

A short-lived groan's what long-time victims wrest
From victors, as from raving Lear to Fool:
A strange tradition, that of the oppressed.

It struck back every time, the chronic jest
Thrown up by those in history's vestibule.
What else should such long servitude attest?

Come each emergency, the back-chat's stressed:
'Cry you mercy, took you for a joint stool'.
A strange tradition, that of the oppressed.

Yet now the process quickens without rest
As new states of emergency unspool.
What else should such long servitude attest?
A strange tradition, that of the oppressed.

4

How reckon but by this new steady state?
Constant emergency defines the real;
Time's passage speeds to match the crisis-rate.

Astute historians strive to estimate
Just what, for us, these crises may reveal.
How reckon but by this new steady state?

Now it's a task for them: to validate
With operative concepts what they feel.
Time's passage speeds to match the crisis-rate.

Carl Schmitt, the fascist jurist, may equate
Emergency with Hitler's doomsday deal:
How reckon but by this new steady state?

But you, historians, shouldn't thus back-date
Oppression just so far as that iron heel.
Time's passage speeds to match the crisis-rate:

Oppression sets the pace, not some fresh spate
Of Nazi bearers of the seventh seal.
'How reckon but by this new steady state?,'

You'll ask, then maybe gather how the fate
Of history saves for you its last appeal.
Time's passage speeds to match the crisis-rate;
How reckon but by this new steady state?

Poetry and Language: Two Villanelles

> . . . the poem that philosophically makes good the defect of languages
> …
>
> No poem is intended for the reader, no picture for the beholder, no symphony for the listener.
>
> 'The Task of the Translator'
>
> The language of nature is comparable to a secret password that each sentry passes to the next in his own language, but the meaning of the password is the sentry's language itself.
>
> *One-Way Street and Other Writings*

1

Always some slight *dérèglement* you sense,
Some defect that compounds the falling-short:
No poem but attempts to recompense.

Enjambement holds the issue in suspense
As prosody and syntax tangle thought.
Always some slight *dérèglement* you sense.

The poem's where that non-coincidence
Shows each new settlement more dearly bought:
No poem but attempts to recompense.

For it's just there the defect may commence,
Where run-on lines and scansion won't comport.
Always some slight *dérèglement* you sense.

The free-verse crew may put up their pretence
Of solving it but that's a last resort:
No poem but attempts to recompense.

A wary ear is our last, best defence,
Fine-whorled so every slightest tremor's caught.
Always some slight *dérèglement* you sense;
No poem but attempts to recompense.

2

The poets channel it, that secret word;
Adamic, though with Eden now long gone
No task of theirs to fathom all they heard.

Some spell prevents it turning quite absurd,
A game of whispers idly chanced upon.
The poets channel it, that secret word.

It's nature's sounds make up for passwords blurred
Through endless rounds of that rapt antiphon:
No task of theirs to fathom all they heard.

Language it was that first and always stirred
Those souls attuned to nature's lexicon:
The poets channel it, that secret word.

Whence the unspoken privilege conferred
As if by post-Edenic organon.
No task of theirs to fathom all they heard.

How else redeem the Babel that's incurred
When each new tower goes up in Babylon?
The poets channel it, that secret word;
No task of theirs to fathom all they heard.

'Pure Language,' Translation, and the Seeds of Time

> It is the task of the translator to release in his own language that pure language that is under the spell of another, to liberate the language imprisoned in a work in his recreation of that work.
>
> 'The Task of the Translator'

> The story is told of an automaton constructed in such a way that it could play a winning game of chess, answering each move of an opponent with a countermove. A puppet . . . . sat before a chessboard placed on a large table. A system of mirrors created the illusion that this table was transparent from all sides. Actually, a little hunchback who was an expert chess player sat inside and guided the puppet's hand . . . . The puppet called 'historical materialism' . . . can easily be a match for anyone if it enlists the services of theology, which today, as we know, is wizened and has to keep out of sight.

> The nourishing fruit of the historically understood contains time as a precious but tasteless seed.
>
> 'Theses on the Philosophy of History'

1

Just what was it I meant by that strange claim?
I must have known back then but could not tell
You now, for love nor money (and whence came
That idiom, that English phrase that fell
Unbidden into place?). Maybe the 'spell'
I spoke of was just such a word-charm cast
By chancing on it at some time long past.

The commentators will mistake my aim
If they suppose 'pure language' to excel,
As I conceive it, any language-game,
Like that, in common use and thus to dwell
In some high realm where words can bid farewell
To mere quotidian commerce and, at last,
Leave *homo loquens* hopelessly outclassed.

2

Don't place me with the mystics, those whose cure
For earthly woes and pains is to accede
To a foredoomed Valhalla where what's 'pure'
Is that which shows an other-worldly creed
As always and already run to seed
Since, like time unredeemed, it lacks all taste
Of lives lost, lives fulfilled, lives gone to waste.

That's why I ask: hold out against the lure
Of such exalted notions, you who read
My broodings on translation to assure
Yourselves that you and I must be agreed.
No language but may tell us, should we heed
Its deepest intimations, how debased
Each word that's not by highest heaven graced.

3

Think of it kindly reader, if you would,
As more to do with words that subtly mime
The motions of the soul – 'soul' understood
As that which, like pure, homogeneous time
Affords what glimpse we have of the sublime
But only once it's borne sweet-bitter fruits
And junked all craving for fake absolutes.

It's what they miss, the mystic brotherhood
Of aspirants whose favoured paradigm
Of blessedness would have their words make good
On that which, like an unvoiced, wordless rhyme,
Enabled the mute vocalist to climb,
As with Munchausen's self-up-hoisting boots,
To heights unreachable by earthly routes.

4

No time, no language, no translation worth
The doing till it throws out such ideas
Of some 'pure language' unalloyed by earth-
Bound tones and sympathies that no one hears

Whose purist yearning for the crystal spheres
Of bodiless communing leaves them prone
To catch no answering echoes but their own.

It's like the doctrine of immaculate birth,
That notion fit for someone who reveres
A mythic purity and perfect dearth
Of all that truckles to the hopes and fears
Still suffered by the sensualist who cheers
Himself with vibrant hymns to flesh and bone
Rather than ditties of no mortal tone.

5

As history invests time's even tread
With stepwise halts, advances, and retreats,
So my 'pure language' shepherds what's unsaid
Between the language-flocks since it defeats
The finest efforts of the logothetes
Until that living history's restored
With those impurities their own reward.

Maybe it's why some readers are misled:
Because, for them, the only tongue that meets
The purist's need is one within the head
Of no mere human wagger – one that beats
The language-bounds as if each word depletes,
Once uttered, a mute wisdom unexplored
By written word or vibrant vocal cord.

6

Not but I'd sometimes yield to its appeal,
That thought of how translation might divine,
Uniquely so, what words must else conceal:
The subtle, occult, almost clandestine
Association that affords a sign,
Unknown to either, of what lies beyond
Yet seals two languages in mutual bond.

Thus far the scholar in me, apt to deal
In allegories that often blurred the line
Twixt secular and sacred in his zeal
For such hermetic readings, poised to mine,
Like Kabbalah, each recondite or fine-
Drawn textual crux whose mysteries respond
To the least wave of his redemptive wand.

7

Then the materialist in me begs I pause,
Take thought, touch earth, and keep it well in mind,
Bert Brecht's advice: that fighting in the cause
Of justice, peace, and liberty's the kind
Of task that may require we leave behind
All lingering in the precincts occupied
By bookish types ensconced from time and tide.

Yet still, at times, the Kabbalist in me draws
My inward gaze to certain texts I find
To offer no such handy exit-clause
From activism or the daily grind
Of party politics that he's got lined
Up ready for me, often though I've tried,
By scholar-wiles, to set that truth aside.

8

Here's what I tell myself for comfort's sake,
Though also hoping that, by happy chance,
My future commentators might just make
More sense of it: that any real advance
On his, Brecht's, terms requires we shouldn't dance
Or match our moves to the game-plan he brings,
That hidden hunchback pulling all the strings.

Let's put the case, for dialectic's sake,
That any game-plan likely to enhance
Mankind's material wellbeing or break
The stranglehold of capitalist high finance
Must free the puppet from that docile trance

Induced by his belief that everything's
Foreknown in each new move the hunchback springs.

9

What's then to strive for, work toward, or win
By our collective efforts to achieve
Those high ideals that find expression in
His writings as in mine? 'The final heave,'
They used to say, but how should we believe
That's our case now with Hitler's puppets trained
To stamp on every scrap of progress gained?

Just think, dear comrade: how can we begin
To win it back, that hard-won ground, if we've
No more to give the workers in Berlin
Who watched the Reichstag burn than make-believe
Scenarios or new tricks up our sleeve
Like that of the automaton whose feigned
Chess-playing flair fools only the crack-brained?

10

For you, theology must always be –
As I said in my somewhat jaundiced style –
A wizened little hunchback we can't see
Since cunningly concealed though all the while
Manipulating, with a Jesuit's guile,
The puppet whose spasmodic moves betray
How rigged it is, the one game he can play.

Please, Comrade Brecht, take this on trust from me:
Those textual labours you're inclined to file
Away marked 'his Kabbalah stuff' are key
To how materialist, anti-mercantile,
And action-primed he is, the bibliophile
Who reads, in what those texts expressly say,
The subtext of a secular judgment-day.

11

Forgive me if I push it on a stage,
The allegory of puppet, hunchback, and –
As I interpret it – this present age
Of end-time-threatening conflict when we stand
In need of guidance from the scholar's hand
So long as that's instructed by the tropes
And tokens of those immemorial hopes.

It's we who might just help you turn the page
On puppet-readings, shrewdly countermand
The victor-chroniclers, and spark the rage
For freedom, truth and justice jointly fanned
By your shrewd *plumpes Denken* and my brand
Of speculative thought whose proper scope's
Best tried alongside you who know the ropes.

A Collector

> O bliss of the collector, bliss of the man of leisure! Of no one has less
> been expected and no one has had a greater sense of well-being than
> a collector. Ownership is the most intimate relationship one can have
> to objects. Not that they come alive in him; it is he who comes alive
> in them.
>
> Collectors are people with a tactical instinct; their experience teaches
> them that when they capture a strange city, the smallest antique shop
> can be a fortress . . . . How many cities have revealed themselves to
> me in the marches I undertook in the pursuit of books!
>
> You should know that in saying this I fully realize that my discussion
> of the mental climate of collecting will confirm many of you in your
> conviction that this passion is behind the times, in your distrust of
> the collector type.
>
> 'Unpacking my Library: A Talk
about Book-Collecting'

How capture that incomparable bliss?
What objects dearer than the ones you own,
Whose gift's to let you say 'they're mine alone,
Yet do not count me covetous in this:
It's not my share of worldly goods that's grown,
Or any rich man's plaything that I'd miss
If poverty or principle said 'kiss
That stuff goodbye, re-read your Marx, atone!'.

Yes, they're commodities, their price assigned
In monetary terms, their shifting worth
As reckoned by the plenitude or dearth
Of suchlike goods, though nowadays defined
As much by how far items of the kind
Float largely free of old-style, down-to-earth
Use-values and, near-magically, give birth
To phantom-hosts, real needs left far behind.

Too smug, too pious, not to mention too
Naïve and simple-minded their retort,
Those bourgeois art-collectors who resort

To Kantian aesthetics as their cue
For saying 'Any value they accrue,
These works, has naught in common with the sort
Of market-value ratio between 'bought'
And 'sold' that bourgeois philistines pursue!'.

For them, it's the particular cachet
That comes of having artworks, or their taste
In art, appear 'disinterested,' based
On pure 'appreciation' (note the way
That word does double service!), so that they
Can deem all 'rich vulgarian' talk misplaced
Since their aesthetic judgement's clearly graced
By each great masterpiece on proud display.

That self-deceiving line's no part of my
Collector's mind-set, passion, craving – call
It what you will but that's not it at all,
The move those mercantile art-fanciers try
To set up as their routine alibi
For sending rival bidders to the wall
While touting their 'disinterest' to forestall
The charge those worsted rivals might apply.

You wrong him, the collector, if you take
His love for those choice objects to entail
The self-same mind-set that would gladly veil
The aims of one perpetually on the make
Behind a theory got up for the sake
Of telling others, and himself, a tale
Where Kant's great edifice, however frail,
Gives wealthy fine-arts patrons their big break.

My books, toys, photographs – to me they stand,
And I to them, in a relation quite
Distinct from that, one where the chief delight
Of ownership is having close at hand
Those objects, trafficked here like contraband,
And such close sharers of my exile's plight
That now their presence grants them, as by right,
Joint welcome to this short-stay wonderland.

I share with them, in turn, the exile's need
For intimacy, that which comes alive
In them as much as me, and which they strive
In vain to conjure up who fail to heed
That tenet of the true collector's creed
Which says: whatever pleasure you derive
From these possessions, know that they survive,
Like you, on terms both parties have agreed.

What's more, don't take the 'leisure' I impute
To those who share with me this sometime state
Of object-centred bliss to indicate
A leisurely existence that might suit
The bourgeois connoisseur, or him whose route
To it starts out with family-wealth of date
And source unverified, and then goes straight
To business deals politely termed 'astute'.

The leisure I'm here speaking of is that
Which comes most often of the opposite
Condition, one whose blessings so befit
Not only me, the scholar marvelling at
The spell they cast on each new habitat,
But us who see how well their exquisite
Affordances are set up to admit
The man with no fixed place to hang his hat.

I say 'well-being,' and I mean the sense
Those objects furnish of beatitudes
Unknown to those for whom it's transient moods
They satisfy, but bringing recompense
Long sought by those for whom they may condense
Fond memories, deeds, life-changes, interludes,
And scenes on which the exiled spirit broods
As if dream-stranded in its own past tense.

There's none whom social expectations rest
As lightly on as he whose unquiet soul
Finds peace in what assigns to him no role
But that of the collector, truly blest
With ownership of objects that attest

His giving up all title to control
Those talismanic qualities whose toll,
If lost, would leave the owner dispossessed.

The packages delivered, books unpacked
From their protective wrappings, jackets bared
And viewed once more – what other joy compared
With that felt when they first arrived intact,
Those mailings self-addressed and left high-stacked
Till I, at last, cast off the spell and aired
Them once again in that new dwelling shared
By books and owner through time-honoured pact.

Yet in their tracking down and capturing
What added bliss, what tactics finely honed,
And what fresh joys enticingly postponed
On sallies that, with any luck, may bring
Fresh acquisitions to the gathering
Of objects – books and paintings – newly owned
And sins of greed or envy now atoned
As the collector's waking dream takes wing.

For there's no state of mind more blissful than
The one that crowns his quest, when times refuse
All comforts else, for just the books to choose
As having a redemptive charge that can,
Like Klee's storm-ravaged Angel, lift the ban
On graven images and disabuse
Those travel-weary souls who else might lose
Their last best chance since exile-time began.

Happiness and Terror

> To be happy is to be able to become aware of oneself without fright.
>
> *One-Way Street and Other Writings*

'Happy the man who . . .': how should I go on?
The times are bad, the psyche won't be fooled.
Let ego-soothers know their day's long gone.

It's by harsh truths the puling ego's schooled.
How else instruct the self in self-defence?
The times are bad, the psyche won't be fooled.

Rough justice – all it's likely to dispense.
Let fools and knaves evade the torment due.
How else instruct the self in self-defence?

Try 'happy the man who's trembled yet come through';
No blessed state that's not been terror-cursed.
Let fools and knaves evade the torment due.

Still, 'it's the torment-free who come off worst' –
That's what we say who've searched our souls in fright:
'No blessed state that's not been terror-cursed'.

We count small blessings, think to ease the blight
With Freud's dark counsel there to call upon.
That's what we say who've searched our souls in fright:
'Happy the man who' . . . : how should I go on?

A Plain Man Looks at the Angel of History

> A Klee painting named 'Angelus Novus' shows an angel looking
> as though he is about to move away from something he is fixedly
> contemplating. His eyes are staring, his mouth is open, his wings
> are spread. This is how one pictures the angel of history. His face is
> turned toward the past. Where we perceive a chain of events, he sees
> one single catastrophe which keeps piling wreckage and hurls it in
> front of his feet. The angel would like to stay, awaken the dead, and
> make whole what has been smashed. But a storm is blowing in from
> Paradise; it has got caught in his wings with such a violence that the
> angel can no longer close them. The storm irresistibly propels him
> into the future to which his back is turned, while the pile of debris
> before him grows skyward. This storm is what we call progress.
>
> 'Theses on the Philosophy of History'

1

'Creative licence' and all that, but still
   It's clear enough, at any rate to my
Sub-Benjaminian subtlety of eye
   And intellect, that no degree of skill

In eking out a limited supply
   Of visual cues could possibly distil,
From the Klee drawing, everything that will,
   In his last text, elude all those who try

To grasp it or communicate its gist
   In terms that go along with this or that
Choice hermeneutic slant. I'd say it's flat
   Impossible, but then perhaps I've missed

The picture's point just as the arcane chat
   Of commentators manages to twist
His words into some view of things that's grist
   To any meaning-mill they're grinding at,

Whether they take the Brechtian line and rate

His Kabbalistic ventures something best
Paused over briefly with a sigh then pressed
  Into materialist service, or translate

His Marxist talk as just the manifest
  And vulgar form of what we'd desecrate
If we gave such mere fads of his the weight
  Of Benjaminian scripture. So the test

Is one that catches them, the exegetes
  Of either party, in an awkward spot
Since his idea of history's master-plot
  Was an unending pile-up of defeats

Whose import, to the angel's eye, was not
  The kind of tragic uplift that completes
Soul's odyssey nor yet the kind that meets
  The standard bunch of requisites for what

Should count as a last-act redemptive turn,
  For some the promised end that signified
God's covenant, for others that which tied
  Their thought in dialectic knots to learn

How a materialist reading might provide
  Them with a better optic to discern
Truths less occult in kind. Thus they'd adjourn
  The end-days so intently prophesied

By readers of a messianic bent
  (Albeit, as the cautious ones require,
Just 'weakly messianic') and aspire
  So shrewdly to translate or reinvent

His Talmudic motifs that their entire
  Text-centred eschatology seemed meant
To herald not so much a non-event
  That still, perversely, set some minds afire

With god-intoxicated thoughts but now
    Its secular equivalent that placed
An unillusioned faith in what embraced
    Such thoughts with a sound Brechtian grasp of how

Their valid kernel might not go to waste
    Once shot of its old shell. So they allow,
Like him, that history may perchance endow
    Ideas long since abandoned or outpaced

By the brisk march of progress with a sense
    That their time's come around at last, or their
Presumed attachment to some *derrière-
    Garde* movement stuck in the pluperfect tense

At last been found to signal, *au contraire*,
    What lay ahead. They managed to condense
Futurity by holding in suspense
    Those rules that drew a *cordon sanitaire*

Between what falls within our rear-view scope
    Of reckoning and what stands so far beyond
Our present grasp that these could 'correspond'
    Only in Baudelaire's sense. Thus shattered hope

Re-constellates to form a fragile bond
    Of trans-world correspondences that cope
With all that debris through a will to trope
    The stubborn literality of *monde*

Quotidienne and thereby show a way
    To keep the whole catastrophe in view,
Yet from an angle so far out of true,
    By all the optic codes, as to convey

How such a slant perspective might imbue
    The angel's vision of a groundhog day
Nightmarishly transformed with that which Klee
    Perhaps meant its beholders to construe

In terms less dire or ominously fraught
    Than Benjamin supplied. No doubting its
Compulsive power to exercise our wits
    By thwarting all the methods we've been taught

To try till we come up with one that fits
    And so dispels our fear of being brought
Up short by an odd piece like this or caught,
    Like shell-shocked angels, in the endless blitz

Of meanings driven by a wind that blows
    From some lost hermeneutic paradise
Where the diviner's art could still suffice
    To bring us peace. The text might then disclose

All kinds of deep enigma to entice
    Our curious minds yet free us from the throes
Of doubt at last, not lead us by the nose
    Until we find some recondite device

By use of which to make his cartoon out
    The very image of apocalypse
Or raise the genre-stakes till fancy tips
    The scales that way. More evidence, no doubt,

Of inability to see what grips
    The eyes and minds of those who talk about
Klee's angel-sketch like this, or like to tout
    Its lines and planes as shot through with the chips

Of messianic time that Benjamin
    Conceived as lying close concealed through all
The debris-strewn millennia in thrall
    To a mystique of progress that had been

(Or so he read those remnants that appal
    The angel) an infernal wind-machine
Whose wrecking powers are most distinctly seen
    By those who know the worst that can befall

Their lives or work. That's why he'd have us shun
    That false idea of homogeneous time,
Or history so conceived, as apt to chime
    All too thought-numbingly with every one

Of those cyclic catastrophes whose prime
    Role – as the victors saw it – was to stun
Hope's clingers-on by stressing the long-run
    Back-catalogue of falls by those who'd climb

To heights where they could spare themselves all sight
    Of grim praeterita and so lose touch
With history full-stop. Else they'd take such
    A Whiggish vantage-point as to invite

His charge of falling back into the clutch
    Of crass triumphalists whose heirs would write
Them out of every history-book despite
    Their having for so long now done so much

To help secure the apostolic line
    Of victors. Let's allow, since it resounds
Throughout his work, that what exceeds the bounds
    Of literal sense will often prove a mine

Where the best digger's one who best expounds
    Not only subtle details that refine
Our textual grasp but truths we should assign
    To the Derridean *hors-texte*. This confounds

All efforts to establish just where tact
    Or good procedure should have fixed the *non
Plus ultra* beyond which the text alone,
    If not in some way adequately backed

By extra-textual sources, formed its own
    Self-referential world that clearly lacked
Firm anchorage in the territory of fact
    Whatever its cross-linkage in the zone

Of intra-textual sense. Let's further yield
　　The point to those who say that, in the case
Of thinkers such as Benjamin, the space
　　Presumed to separate life and text is sealed

Against the very doctrines that would base
　　Their separation on the truths revealed
By lives that, unlike his, lay unconcealed
　　Or not at every stage compelled to face

Such threats of inward or external source
　　As otherwise might drive him to the brink
Of terminal despair. Still those who think
　　To see prefigured in his texts the course

His life took in its last few weeks, and link
　　His life-text to Klee's image, may endorse
No less an error than the strict divorce
　　Insisted on by purist types who'd shrink

The hedgehog text secure within its rolled-
　　Up prickly tenement and then enjoy
An unrestricted freedom to employ
　　Those same techniques to shrink and then enfold

The world safe in the text lest it destroy
　　Their fine-tuned instruments. Yet readers sold
On life-and-times and captive to the hold
　　Of Klee's mesmeric angel should alloy

The elements that go to allegorize
　　Those last death-haunted weeks by turning back
To ask if Klee's creation might not lack,
　　Judged simply on what's there before one's eyes,

The sorts of quality whose sum could stack
　　Up close to what he'd have us recognise
In its blank gaze. More likely this supplies
　　The exegetes with just sufficient slack

To compensate the angel's deficit
  With value-added features that might lend
Themselves, thus amply viewed, to the chief end
  These readers have in mind of bringing it

And Benjamin's life-history to blend
  By text-osmosis. Should it not submit
At first attempt, the very lack of fit
  Between Klee's image and the fragments penned

By Benjamin about it goes to make
  More working space for just that hybrid mode
Of commentary whose aim is to decode,
  Through every mazy detour it might take,

The language of analogies he showed,
  In Baudelaire, to link the wide-awake
Of consciousness with images that break
  Through from oneiric regions and explode

All the codes and conventions we perceive
  To constitute the real. Still we'd do well
Not to fall quite so much beneath the spell
  Of Klee's beguiling image, but take leave

To query some of what they have to tell,
  Those dreamworld-emissaries, and retrieve
Only some select part of what they weave
  From history's stray threads. Else we may dwell

Too fixedly upon it and become,
  Ourselves, so many angels left behind
Yet driven forward by some brute impulse blind
  To past and future, or possessed by some

Resistless drive that leaves the reeling mind
  Deprived of motive or intent to plumb
Its own inchoate depths and therefore dumb
  To give their dumbstruck angel voice or find

Some apter idiom to convey what's past
    Its gobsmacked power to tell. Just look once more
At Klee's *ange de nos jours* and then, if you're
    Still one by whom image and text are cast

In co-star roles, then by all means ignore
    This (you'll think) vain endeavour to contrast
Those roles by striving – as he'd say – to blast
    A hole in that too intimate rapport

Between the two. If, on the other hand,
    Your inclinations run *contre Saint-Beuve*
For something like Proust's reasons, it may serve
    To help you more resolvedly withstand

The knack they have of touching a raw nerve,
    Those reading-protocols that take a bland
Or rough-hewn image linked to an unplanned
    Event or chance catastrophe, then swerve

Into a realm of figural excess
    Where last days and late writings each assume
The sense of some far-back prefigured doom.
    This no such graven image could express

Unless one so unformed that you could zoom
    Right in yet be no better placed to guess
What the thing signified, which points to stress,
    Or even – like some garbled code – for whom

It's meant. My point is, Benjamin was far
    Ahead of his interpreters in just
The strategies required if we're to trust
    His subtle exegete, while there's a bar

(Or should be) on our craving to encrust
    Those texts and images that bear the scar
Of lives destroyed or ruined with what are,
    In truth, projections of a kind we must

Put down to our own wishes rather than
    Project onto the author's *vouloir-dire*
Or life *hors-texte*. This might apply if we're
    So eminently well-equipped to scan

Their import that there's no life/text frontier
    To cross, or need for us to heed the ban
On any misplaced notion that we can,
    By gift of divination or by sheer

Telepathy, gain insight such as struck
    A note of dodgy practice with the likes
Of 'old' New Critics, and more lately strikes
    The same false note to those who'll have no truck

With an *echt*-Heideggerian turn that hikes
    Its self-ascribed ability to pluck
Deep meanings out while others remain stuck
    With surface sense, till some gross error spikes

Its hermeneutic guns. For it's the mix
    Of life-historic truth with allegory's
Long-licensed swerves from it that render his
    Example not the best by which to fix

Our working notion of how history's
    Or life's demands might stipulate what ticks
The vital boxes, rather than the tricks
    Of *n*-fold exegesis that some whiz

Life-allegorist might make out to contain,
    In nuce, every episode of note
Which their close-reading skills may then promote
    By textual magic to a higher plane.

2

A far cry, this, from what the Brechtians wrote
    In their Marx-tutored efforts to restrain
The angel's flight by hitting on the vein
    Of *plumpes Denken* aptest to connote

Their message that, wherever fancy's bred,
    Its offspring yield their secrets only when
Pressed to reveal, beyond the author's ken,
    Such meanings as could properly be read

By good materialists alone, and then
    Just those of them not prone to be misled
By each new allegoric go-ahead
    From that deceiving elf. Compare again

Klee's image with the commentary it drew
    From this most rapt and erudite among
The many who've been drawn, enticed, or stung
    To write about it, and you'll get a clue

As to why some brave exegetes have clung
    To literal sense against the larger crew
Of intertextual lemon-squeezers who,
    From ancient times, habitually flung

Such hermeneutic caution to the wild,
    Shape-shifting winds that tangle all the codes,
Mix up historical and fictive modes
    Of discourse, and – through meaning-strata piled

Heaven-high – ensure that pious labour loads
    Each rift with sacred lore. The Fathers styled
Their four-fold method that which reconciled
    Our tongues post-Babel through God-granted nodes

Of mutual comprehension that relieved,
    From time to time, the cacophonic din
And promised to undo old Adam's sin
    (Plus the tower-building exploit that so peeved

A jealous God) by speech-events akin
    To those that Benjamin himself conceived
As bearers of the one gift that reprieved
    Our fallen language-state. They helped us win,

Like his authentic poet-allegorist,
    A post-Edenic glimpse of how things stood
Back then while no tight bonds of nationhood
    Or speech-community contrived to twist

Our meanings out of true. Since now there could,
    He thought, be no sound method to assist
Translators in attaining what they missed
    Nine times in ten, and brought off only should

Some miracle permit, the task they had,
    In Benjamin's hard teaching, was to pass
Through and beyond the sense-refracting glass
    Of language, like the magic writing-pad

Of Freud's analogy, and – what they'd class,
    Those Brechtians, just another quirk to add
On his Talmudic debit side or fad
    Picked up through Scholem's influence, alas –

By that means come as near as we're allowed,
    Us post-lapsarians, to the language-game
That Adam played. This gave each beast a name
    By which it stood distinct amongst the crowd,

Since name and nature signified the same
    Divine intent that all things be endowed
With just that *haeccitas* that did them proud
    By showing how their nomination came

Through God's decree and not – *pace* the rule
    That holds for mortal languages – as laid
Down by those proto-structuralists who made
    Of it a strict requirement in their school

That one maintain no sense can be conveyed
    Except by use of that all-purpose tool,
The arbitrary sign. This way the pool
    Of communal-linguistic usage paid

Its debt to structures far outside the reach
  Of conscious grasp or way beyond the pale
Of what might figure in the fictive tale
  Contrived by those who far preferred to teach

(Like him at times) a mystic doctrine stale
  Through centuries of abuse. Adamic speech,
As Benjamin conceived it, rendered each
  Of structuralism's tenets sure to fail

The test of language-faith which said that no
  Mere act of meaning-transference across
Two languages, however small the loss
  Of literal sense involved, could ever show

That third dimension shadowed by the gloss
  The allegorist supplies. Such claims may go,
For scholars, way beyond what's apropos
  But for text-gleaners separate the dross

Of literal gist from the rare gleam of pure
  Or pre-discursive language that reveals,
To souls attuned, a sense that sense conceals
  Since the forked tongues of men work to obscure

What so exceeds their compass or repeals
  The law of plain intent. That helped assure
Loquacious mortals – when the talking cure
  Misfired – that good communication heals

The wounds of fractured sense without the least
  Assistance from those peddlers of abstruse
Hermetic doctrine who might so seduce
  Our waking minds that all the bits we'd pieced

Together in some roughly fit-for-use
  Communicative order promptly ceased
To signify at all. Then some off-piste
  Interpretation or some fast-and-loose

Analogy drove thought clean off the tracks
    And into a lost-soul-frequented maze
Of allegoric meanings. These might craze
    The seeker's wits or else so greatly tax

Their hermeneutic skills that every phrase
    Becomes one more inscription in the wax
That holds, as in Freud's writing-pad, the stacks
    Of past inscriptions that our minds erase

Yet whose material traces still engrave
    The archive of what memory retains
At some unconscious level. Here the brain's
    Ancestral wiring bids it always save

For future use whatever it disdains
    To memorise or even seeks to stave
Off at all costs where the occurrence gave
    So great a shock that now it too much pains

Remembrance to record. That's why I say,
    Or said way back when this thing started out,
That probably the best, most useful route
    (US pronunciation) to essay

Such questions is by taking leave to doubt,
    Contra the commentators, whether Klee
In any real sense managed to display
    The tiniest part of what his deep-devout

Ekphrastic *Uebersetzer* sought to parse
    In terms so eloquent that they provoked,
In turn, the kind of meta-gloss that yoked
    Its speculative compass to the stars

Of some remote sense-constellation cloaked
    In figural deep space. This firmly bars
The way for those whose 20/20 mars
    Their chance of having egos nicely stroked

By coming up with an eccentric slant
　　On meanings or appearances that makes
Of their strabismic gaze just what it takes
　　To see things clear or, like his angel, grant

A visionary power to raise the stakes
　　Of exegetic faith. Thus they implant,
In the more literal-minded – those who can't
　　Quite get their eyes or heads around what breaks

With all the rules – a notion that it's their
　　Defect of brain or vision that's the cause
Of this, or some endemic range of flaws
　　On their part that must shoulder the main share

Of blame. Yet if one thought should give us pause
　　In saying this, or bid us take more care
Before we heirs of Benjamin declare
　　On his side of the question, it's that clause

In all such mystical or cryptic creeds
　　That makes a watchword, then a shibboleth
Of what, if known, becomes the very breath
　　Of life but, if unknown, sends him who reads

In ignorance straight off to dusty death,
　　Or (less dramatically) for special-needs
Sense-ampliative training which then breeds,
　　In some, such devious spells as drove Macbeth

To that conclusion.

3

　　　　　Let's ourselves conclude,
　　More hopefully, that there's room to extend
Our critical horizons and suspend
　　Those cautionary maxims that obtrude

Too much on our ambitions to transcend
　　The commonplace without things getting skewed

To such a point that only ultra-clued-
    Up allegorists can hope to comprehend

What's going on. Then all the rest are lumped,
    Like the unclued-up types who, Jesus said,
Lacked ears to hear, with those who lose the thread
    Of some soul-saving parable that stumped

Their feeble intellects since poorly read,
    Or read in ignorance of that which trumped
The overt gist and so cast those who plumped
    For literal sense amongst the living dead

Of cloth-eared infidels. It's this that throws
    A sharper light on Benjamin's wire-drawn
Klee-commentary and how it's apt to spawn
    Yet wilder flights of fantasy from those

Who think that understanding starts to dawn
    Only at that far point where reading goes
Beyond the utmost limits of plain-prose
    Interpretation and becomes a pawn

In some text-game more erudite by half
    Than any trial of wits that might result
From sights fixed wisely short of those occult
    Meaning-coordinates way off the graph

Of shared intent. So, rather than exult
    In getting the last anagogic laugh
Or writing literal sense's epitaph,
    These thinkers tend more often to consult,

If not the 'common reader,' then her near
    Relation who reads closely and in full
Cognizance of how words sometimes can pull
    New wonders up from thought's unconscious sphere,

Yet also of how this can pull the wool
    Over the eyes of allegorists who'd peer

Asquint or upside-down at texts for fear
    Of acting like the hermeneutic bull

In meaning's china-shop. What may have done
    Its share to pile sky-high the wreckage hurled
At the angel's feet, to keep its wings unfurled,
    And give the wind called 'progress' power to stun

Or mesmerise its gaze is what lay curled,
    Like agenbite of inwit, in each one
Of those choice texts whose eisogetes had spun
    Around them such an intertextual world

Of gloss and commentary that nothing seemed
    Revision-proof enough to stand against
The blitz of meaning-fragments that commenced
    Its sense-unravelling work each time they dreamed

Of some transcendent vision that dispensed
    With modes of discourse so obliquely themed
As further to fragment the mass that streamed
    From paradise. So if he finds condensed

In Klee's *unheimlich* angel such a deal
    Of pent significance, perhaps that's less
Because the thing has such power to compress
    Multum in parvo than in hopes that he'll

Have some small chance to parlay the distress
    That comes of knowing this *Glasperlenspiel*
A game forever lost with no appeal
    To any saving vision that might bless

Us finally by showing how the storm
    Of progress must at some point cease to rage
Or, by some very marvel of backstage
    Plot-fixing, grant intelligible form

To that mere piling-up of age-on-age
    Calamities that constitutes the norm

As viewed from any place within the swarm
    Of tempest-driven debris. Let us gauge

How deep it was, that allegory that held
    Him fascinated, like the death's-head tropes
Of *Trauerspiel,* by seeing how he copes
    Not only with such life-events as spelled

Defeat for all his dearest private hopes
    But also with the history that compelled
His angel to a *Rückwärtsblick* that quelled
    Even the flickering faith of one who gropes

For long-range consolation. What he shared
    With the skull-gazers whose unhinged pursuit
Of vengeance left them and their victims mute,
    By the last act, to say why we'd been spared

No devilish atrocity *en route*
    To that denouement is the thought that there'd
Be something fake about a plot that squared
    With just desert or turned out to commute

Our final verdict on the bloody farce
    To a more meaningful since tragic sort
Of moral uplift. Though this might comport
    More readily with sentiments that pass

For truly human it would so distort
    The moribund revenger's *coup de grâce*
That we'd have just a Beckett-type impasse
    Of failed apocalypse that fell far short

Of such redemptive power. The angel's curse,
    It then appears, is that which figures all
Our lives and histories as one long-haul
    Deluded odyssey from bad to worse,

A message more than likely to appal
    Those thinkers temperamentally averse

To such gloom-mongering but which some rehearse,
  As if apotropaically, to stall

Catastrophe and turn the thing around
  At last. Then a few fragments might be snatched
From chaos and, by patient sifting, matched
  With a few others so as to propound

A view of things not too securely latched
  To hope's rickety wagon nor yet bound,
By gloomy predilection, to confound
  All thoughts of progress with a doctrine hatched

By *Kulturpessimismus* from the wreck
  Of the old Europe Pound once called 'a bitch
Gone in the teeth'. So if he chose to ditch
  Its cherished values as not up to spec

And, at the Spanish frontier, unhitch
  His own life-burdened wagon where the trek
Ran into one last fatal border-check,
  Then it's Klee's mute apocalypse to which

We dwellers in the aftermath had best
  Direct our not too sharply focused gaze
If we're to grasp why such communiqués
  As his and Benjamin's are not addressed

To expert eyes well practised in the ways
  Of eisogesis but to those unblessed
With any special skill save that expressed
  By everything about it that betrays

The angel's having nothing to impart
  Like news of virgin births or other themes
In arch-seraphic style. Rather than streams
  Of light celestial tricked out by art

Into some true epiphany that seems
  To find its way to every viewer's heart,

Klee simply says: no vision here apart
　　From an angel-shaped thing that neither screams,

Like Munch's shocker, nor assumes a look
　　Of rapture whether sacred or profane,
Nor, like a Buddha-face, seems to contain
　　All these brave opposites since it can brook

Their discord undisturbed. More it's the plain
　　Uncomprehending blankness that so shook
Klee's expert draughtsmanship and left the book
　　Of life, for Benjamin, a text-domain

Where allegory contrived to cock a snook
　　At any symbol-seer who hoped to gain
Such insight as the angel sought in vain
　　Through every tropic twist the storm-path took.

Unforgettable

One might, for example, speak of an unforgettable life or moment even if all men had forgotten it. If the nature of such a life or moment required that it be unforgotten, that predicate would imply not a falsehood but merely a claim unfulfilled by men, and probably also a reference to a realm in which it is fulfilled: God's remembrance.

'The Task of the Translator'

The only historian capable of fanning the spark of hope in the past is the one who is firmly convinced that even the dead will not be safe from the enemy if he is victorious.

'Theses on the Philosophy of History'

1

Should the Recording Angel not have wings?
The memorable may not come to mind.
Time-sensitive, the vital news she brings.

The past deed flashes up, the image springs;
Too long we lived forgetful, aspect-blind.
Should the Recording Angel not have wings?

By her swift flights alone remembrance clings
To call-signs that hiatus left behind.
Time-sensitive, the vital news she brings.

Else they'll be lost, those *Jetztzeit* tokenings,
Or lost to us who've bearings yet to find.
Should the Recording Angel not have wings?

A broken music to our ears she sings,
Though future-charged when punctually divined.
Time-sensitive, the vital news she brings.

And yet, of this be sure: that everything's
Recorded, every past act truth-consigned.
Should the Recording Angel not have wings?
Time-sensitive, the vital news she brings.

2

Who'll say alms for oblivion leaves no debt?
They err who think 'forgotten' means 'clean slate'.
What's unforgettable we may forget.

Those lives, deaths, moments, deeds we should regret
Or view with pride – they've no fixed recall-date.
Who'll say alms for oblivion leaves no debt?

We'd be truth's sole key-holders should we set
Its scope and limits by our memory-state:
What's unforgettable we may forget.

Think rather it's truth's standard must be met
If anything's to set our errors straight.
Who'll say alms for oblivion leaves no debt?

For mere forgetfulness may mask those yet-
Un-rediscovered truths that lie in wait.
What's unforgettable we may forget,

But should keep that in mind so never let
Hope's fragile witness fall to Pyrrho's fate.
Who'll say alms for oblivion leaves no debt?
What's unforgettable we may forget.

Angelus Novus

(These villanelles can be read as an extended ekphrastic commentary on the passage from Benjamin's 'Theses on the Philosophy of History' where he offers an allegorical reading of Paul Klee's now-famous drawing/water-colour image *Angelus Novus* (1920). For extended citation of the Benjamin text, see headnote, p. 80.

1

Face backward where the wreckage piles sky-high.
That storm's called 'progress,' so my 'Theses' said.
Unfold your wings, but do not think to fly.

No use now for your expert weather-eye,
Nor for your flying skills: you'd best instead
Face backward where the wreckage piles sky-high.

There's too much debris cluttering the sky,
Along with parts by other angels shed.
Unfold your wings, but do not think to fly.

No second thoughts: however hard you try
To fold them flat the gale keeps them outspread.
Face backward where the wreckage piles sky-high.

Some say it blows from paradise, but I
Think that's from some Kabbalah-text they read.
Unfold your wings, but do not think to fly.

No point postdating when things went awry,
Though it's the kind of mythic tale we're fed.
Face backward where the wreckage piles sky-high.

On every scale this lesson must apply:
Be not by thoughts of Eden so misled.
Unfold your wings, but do not think to fly.
Face backward where the wreckage piles sky-high.

2

The storm's still raging, that we can't deny:
Through wings it whistles fit to wake the dead.
End-times or not, there's some disaster nigh.

Paradise lost is our stock alibi;
It's putting dates to doomsday we most dread.
The storm's still raging, that we can't deny.

No primal bliss, nor reason to ask why.
Back then catastrophe lay far ahead.
End-times or not, there's some disaster nigh.

Still there's the question: what can justify
This stretching of the parable's fine thread?
The storm's still raging, that we can't deny.

Who'll blame the exegetes when they decry
My want of such angelic fear to tread?
End-times or not, there's some disaster nigh.

Gershom alone might see the point of my
Thus conjuring angel-visions long since fled.
The storm's still raging, that we can't deny.

A lingering hope to live before I die
Is why those visions are my daily bread.
End-times or not, there's some disaster nigh;
The storm's still raging, that we can't deny.

Redeeming the Time: Benjamin *contra* Eliot

> A people without history
> Is not redeemed from time, for history is a pattern
> Of timeless moments. So, while the light fails
> On a winter's afternoon, in a secluded chapel
> History is now and England.
>> T.S. Eliot, 'Little Gidding'

> The general point of view may be described as classicist in literature, royalist in politics, and Anglo-Catholic in religion.
>> Eliot, Preface to *For Lancelot Andrewes*

> Tradition is a matter of much wider significance. It cannot be inherited, and if you want it you must obtain it by great labour. . . . This historical sense, which is a sense of the timeless as well as of the temporal and of the timeless and of the temporal together, is what makes a writer traditional.
>> Eliot, 'Tradition and the Individual Talent'

> There is no document of civilization which is not at the same time a document of barbarism.

> History is the subject of a structure whose site is not empty, homogeneous time, but time filled with the presence of the now (*Jetztzeit*).

> Whoever has emerged victorious participates to this day in the triumphal procession in which the present rulers step over those who are prostrate.
>> Benjamin, 'Theses on the Philosophy of History'

Almost I might succumb to it, the tone
Of grave, hard come-by wisdom, as of one
'Expert beyond experience,' in your own*
Much earlier words, or as of young Jack Donne
Already preaching coffin-cased, outrun
By time and late regrets, resolved, like you,
To miss no chance of spoiling any fun

---

* The 'you' addressed in the poem is Eliot, not Benjamin.

His auditors might think their living due
And have them shuddering in the chilliest pew.

I think of your late summa, 'Four Quartets,'
Much cited, much admired, much used to speak,
Vicariously, of those same late regrets
By readers, exegetes, all those who'd seek
Admission through it to a high mystique
Of faith, tradition, Englishness, and all
Such fine accoutrements – the more antique
The better – guaranteed to hold in thrall
Those driven to frequent your well-stocked stall.

Then, to dispel the holy mystery
Around those thoughts, it's Walter Benjamin's
'Theses on the Philosophy of History'
That, oddly, come to mind as one begins
To see what's going on, how your verse spins
A mystical conception of time past,
Present, and future on a creed that twins
Deceptively with Benjamin's, though cast
Far back in time to hold time's motion fast.

Not for the hierophant of Christian faith,
Of classicism, monarchy, and such-
Like orthodoxies premised on 'He saith'
As final word, lest tossed into the clutch
Of alien gods – not yours the saving touch
Of Benjamin's *rücksichtlich* angel, wings
Outspread, storm-driven back, and with no crutch
Of faith to lean on, yet in hope that springs,
If not eternal, then from timely things.

For it's the *Jetztpunkt* moments, those that flash
Up suddenly, unlooked-for, in the flow
Of homogeneous time, or cut a dash
Where long defeat and caution said 'Go slow,
Or give up now' – it's those that may just show
The hearkeners to your penitential mode
Of history-reckoning how things might go
If some new-found old memory tweaks the code
And hope relives a long-past episode.

It's 'homogeneous time' that your verse wants
To consecrate, a time devoid of just
That brief redemptive interval that haunts
The immemorial sleep of those who must,
At all costs, not permit themselves to trust
Such sempiternal longings lest they get,
At length, to kid themselves this mortal dust
Lays claim to a futurity whose debt
To victims past stands unredeemed as yet.

That 'Four Quartets' verse-music: what's the tune
If not one pitched precisely to deny
Those Benjaminian thoughts as picayune,
Mere products of his hoping to get by
On earthbound angel-wings, unfit to fly
Because confined by secular decree
To gazing backward at a ravaged sky
While hooded angel-eyes no longer see
Beyond the piled historical debris.

Past, present, future – each, for you, a phase
Or mode of 'empty, homogeneous time,'
That specious past-made-present that betrays,
For Benjamin, the merely punctual chime
Of history's dull carillon, the rhyme
That comes around routinely, or event
Whose happening lacks the latent power to prime
Remembrance with a charge that maybe went
For nothing once yet still remains unspent.

'Learn to sit still,' you say, 'contain your souls
In Christian patience, know that time exceeds
Our mortal grasp while grace alone paroles
This living interval, supplies our needs
For spirit-sustenance, and sternly pleads
We not go whoring "after strange gods" that tempt
The docile soul with God-forsaking creeds,
Or bid us think shrewd counsel might pre-empt
His judgment, leave us sinners guilt-exempt'.

For you, the 'still point of the turning world'
Is time suspended, time that's static-still,

Since there's no history but what's unfurled
Past-present-future as might best fulfil
God's purpose, leaving naught for human will
To compass or project beyond the late
Acceptance, on our part, that not until
Our angel lifts its eyes to contemplate
Things timeless can that tumult once abate.

Not so for Benjamin: his angel stares
Back horrified, fixated, as the heap
Of wreckage grows, as every storm-gust bears
Him back resistlessly, and as the creep
Of fascism looks certain to hold cheap
All erstwhile gains and thereby to defile
All future hopes – yet he'll be sure to keep
On watch for glimmerings in the wreckage-pile
That flash the signal: go that extra mile!

What's your 'tradition'? Simply one that gains
Canonic power to tell us all what's what,
The masterworks that Benjamin arraigns
As barbarism's cultural master-shot,
Its whip-hand that instructs the other lot,
Nay-sayers to that sacrosanct regime,
In ways to voice dissent yet show it's not
So radical or vocal as to seem
Signed up full-time with the opponent's team.

'No document of civilization that's
Not also one of barbarism' – thus
He phrased it, without queasy caveats
Or get-out clauses for good guys like us
Or him, the sort quite willing to discuss
Such awkward topics just so long as they're
In line for culture-kudos or the plus-
Points due to anyone who claims a share
In making culture-clones more self-aware.

Your role? To give thanks as the victor's spoils
Are carried in procession, as they ride

106

Rejoicing over millions whose long toils
Have made that triumph possible, and hide
Its monstrous roots by taking well in stride
The cruelty, pain, and suffering it took
To keep the wealthy philistines onside,
Keep most folk thinking 'culture' a closed book,
And keep the plebs away by hook or crook.

'This storm's what we call progress,' so he said,
That victim of a culture gone as far
As any on the hellish path that led
From Beethoven to Belsen, from all-star
Composers, poets, thinkers to the scar
On its and every conscience left to grieve
At just how deeply intertwined they are,
Those histories, and how far we misconceive
The work of art as fitted to unweave

That fateful pattern. Not for you, his sense
Of the dark signature that underwrote
Each masterpiece, each covert recompense
For brute regimes that had us by the throat,
Or each Arnoldian touchstone one could quote
To pay the needful homage, like those lines
Of yours that so beguilingly promote
A history-lite nostalgia that combines
Verse-music with a tour of scenic shrines

To High Church doctrine, monarchy, good taste,
And – unremarked – all that it took to force
Compliance on the mob. Who better placed
Than you to track that culture back to source
And quit the States for England where divorce
Of one kind or another soon became
Your big theme, from the contumelious course
Of church and state post-Henry to – the same
Thing parsed in lit-crit terms – the split you'd blame

On a deep-laid *dérèglement* between
Thought and emotion such as came about

When schism rose to fracture what had been
Their union up until that tiresome rout,
The English Civil War. And should we doubt
The truth of this, or count it just a flight
Of retro-reverie you're keen to tout,
Then there's your 'Four Quartets' to put us right
By having those rent faculties unite

In a new poet, one who'll up the ante
By picking fresh precursors till the norm
Goes back another age, from Donne to Dante,
And takes the curiously imposing form
Of one whose soul's more troubled by the swarm
Of modern heresies than any blitz
Or thunderclap delivered by the 'storm
From paradise' that Benjamin outfits
With terrors to beware of when it hits

Your image. A string quartet whose chief
Role here's to match the rapt, slow-moving dance
Of practised partners, weaving each motif
Into that timeless pattern where a glance
Exchanged gives notice players will advance,
Retard, adjust their tempi to maintain
A deep unchanging order, and entrance
The listener lest some sudden key-shift strain
Their nerves or Beethovenian storm disdain

Such playing-styles, such striving to ensure
That history's bland continuum not succumb
To elemental shocks. How then secure
Your line, preserve that sole imperium
From Virgil, Dante, Shakespeare, Donne, and some
Choice candidates thereafter down to your
Discreetly muffled strategy to drum
Them out, those wounded in a bygone war
That fractured sensibilities and tore

A polity apart, then left to you
The task of setting poetry on track

Once more. Yours, too, the critic's slanted view
Of how and why they went off-course way back,
A mythic tale that makes up for its lack
Of documentary substance with a shrewd
Or well-turned catchphrase and a handy knack
For passing off, with po-faced certitude,
Some odd idea that matched your current mood.

'All time is unredeemable,' you say,
And make it so by leaving us perplexed
In toils of temporal paradox the way
It left you, reading F. H. Bradley – vexed
Yet fascinated, mental muscles flexed
On puzzles deep enough to tax the mind
Of Harvard graduates – but then, 'what next?,'
Except to show how faith alone assigned
An exit-point from logic's double-bind.

'State of emergency': that's how he turns
Your message on its head, requires we junk
That fideist response, switch our concerns
From dead eternity to this, our chunk
Of living-time when only those who funk
The angel's ultimatum need to cower
In the cathedral close of Lowell's skunk-
Hour quarter where the penitential hour
Is that which strikes as gothic demons lour

Or fascists seize their chance to claim a stake
In history. Once dragged to that inert,
Eventless realm no counter-force can make
A lasting mark, no contraflow divert
The storm-tossed flying debris and assert
What you'd much rather have your verse conceal:
The truth that only angels on alert
For fake time-paradoxes can reveal
How they've connived at history's raw deal.

'If all time is eternally present,' then
'All time is unredeemable' – they miss

The import there, your readers, though the yen
For thought-subduing cadences makes this
More likely as you turn to reminisce
On past loves, seasons, roses that dehisce
In chapel-gardens, and the sense that you've
Regained, at times, the momentary bliss
That comes of having these high musings prove
The wisdom of your transatlantic move.

Yet ponder them, those lines, and maybe you'll
Just glimpse what Benjamin held out against
In thought's old ruse to sanctify the rule
Of those old powers whose tightening grip he sensed
Behind idealist systems that dispensed
With history, conquest, suffering, and the brute
Or – maybe – the redemptive charge condensed
In Klee's *Angelus Novus*. Battered, mute,
Storm-harried, wind-bewildered, destitute,

And shell-shocked, yet it witnesses how sheer
Endurance through the ages, soul's distress
At body's indigence, and body's fear
Of soul's exactions might one day redress
That worst of wrongs as bodies coalesce
With souls. Then history will give the lie
To those, like you, with voices tuned to bless
The mystic status quo that said: comply,
And you'll have done your bit to satisfy

An order whose transcendent timelessness
Affords an always timely alibi
For celebrants in waiting to profess
The articles of faith, Anglican-High
Or crypto-Catholic (potential fly
In your anointment). You've a wicked ear
For fakery, we know, and a sharp eye
For shoddy spirit-goods, but that austere
Façade lets on what strange gods you revere.

What Price the Muse?

There is no muse of philosophy, and there is also no muse of translation. They are not, however, philistine, as sentimental artistic folk would like to think. For there is a philosophical genius, whose essential characteristic is the longing for the language that is announced in translation.

True translation is transparent: it does not obscure the original, does not stand in its light, but rather allows pure language, as if strengthened by its own medium, to shine even more fully on the original.

'The Task of the Translator'

Note: this is a dialogue-poem about inspiration ('the muse') and the place it should properly occupy – or not – in relation to philosophy and translation. The two conflicting viewpoints are distinguished by the absence or presence of italics, though their differences should emerge clearly enough as the dialogue goes along. It ends very emphatically on one side.

1

Shall reason heed the flighty muse?
What need for inspiration there?
Read Kant, let intellect beware
The prophet's tone, the mystic's ruse.

Too easily their spells enthuse
Weak minds with volumes of hot air.
Shall reason heed the flighty muse?
What need for inspiration there?

Philosophers should query whose
That voice, those words, that fraudster's flair,
And disown any thought that their
Ideas fall in with suchlike views.
Shall reason heed the flighty muse?
What need for inspiration there?

2

Her blessings why should you refuse?
Can reason's source not dwell elsewhere?
Why should you then exert such care
To veto inspiration's dues?

It's reason's better part you lose
By upping intuition's share.
Her blessings why should you refuse?
Can reason's source not dwell elsewhere?

No, it's the trickster's way you choose,
The way of charlatans, the snare
Of those with lofty words to spare
But none a thinker would excuse.

3

It's our wise counsel you abuse,
You heirs of Descartes and Voltaire!
We suffer your ill will and bear
Your taunts for breaking false taboos.

It's these our gifts you'd better use
Than cast aside, all unaware:
It's our wise counsel you abuse,
You heirs of Descartes and Voltaire!

Once more the 'inner light' renews,
Brings thoughts divine and visions rare,
Then new creeds harshly doctrinaire
That soon make hideous headline news.
It's our wise counsel you abuse,
You heirs of Descartes and Voltaire!

4

Translator, bid your muse retire!
Stay close, stay literal, stay true.
Resist what she would have you do
To sate her own perverse desire.

It's mine to say, not up to you,
What rendering these lines require.
Translator, bid your muse retire!
Stay close, stay literal, stay true.

O poem, why should I aspire
To do no more than take my cue
From your demand that I should hew
To rules that suit a pen-for-hire.
Translator, bid your muse retire!
Stay close, stay literal, stay true.

5

Ephebe, call down no muse of fire,
Nor jump the prime-creator queue.
No need: quite willing to eschew
Such sins and skip your rightful ire!

Still, should I risk a trope or two
That owns the muse as prime supplier . . .
Ephebe, call down no muse of fire,
Nor jump the prime-creator queue

. . . then, poet, it's my own high-flyer
Risk that I take, not one to slew
Your high renown by seeking through
Misprision to see it expire.
Ephebe, call down no muse of fire,
Nor jump the prime-creator queue.

6

And yet, why should I aim no higher
Than that slave-role you'd hold me to?
Why not some strong-revisionist coup
That clean o'er-leaps your low trip-wire?

Your plea, translator, shows you rue
Your service-task, resent my prior . . .
And yet, why should I aim no higher
Than that slave-role you'd hold me to?

. . . as I just said, resent my prior
And rightful claim to lay down who
Can best make up the descant crew
Amongst my readers' votive choir.
And yet, why should I aim no higher
Than that slave-role you'd hold me to?

7

Read Benjamin if you'd know why
You each require the muses' aid,
You Dichter-Denker *so afraid*
Of what might leave you high and dry!

Their inspiration's all that made
Your poems sing, your ideas fly.
Read Benjamin if you'd know why
You each require the muses' aid.

It's their good grace you're succoured by.
How else were those trouvailles *conveyed,*
The leap of thought that made the grade,
The metaphor that touched the sky?
Read Benjamin if you'd know why
You each require the muses' aid.

8

So you, translator, don't fight shy
Of your share in the accolade:
No cause to think the work's betrayed
If risks, like recompense, run high.

Strict word-for word must needs evade
The task he sought to clarify,
So you, translator, don't fight shy
Of your share in the accolade.

A realm no tongue can occupy,
'Pure language,' where the frontiers fade,
All interlingual debts are paid,

Yet fixed exchange-rates don't apply.
So you, translator, don't fight shy
Of your share in the accolade.

9

Think then of what a far, far cry
It is from mind's quotidian trade
In words or thoughts when both cascade
To knock its trusty props awry.

What else but inspiration swayed
That mind to cast off habit's tie?
Think then of what a far, far cry
It is from mind's quotidian trade.

Read in his texts how close they lie
For Benjamin, those roles he played
Of poet, scholar, and arcade-
Struck promeneur *with questing eye.*
Think then of what a far, far cry
It is from mind's quotidian trade.

10

Then you may tell the philistine
He goes astray in both respects,
Not seeing how the muse connects
Deep-lying thoughts and singing line.

Call 'muse' the point where intellect's
And intuition's gifts combine;
Then you may tell the philistine
He goes astray in both respects.

That point may likewise help define
Just where translation intersects
Their conjoint planes and so reflects
Pure language, glass of the divine.
Then you may tell the philistine
He goes astray in both respects.

Beyond the Pleasure-Principle

Something different is disclosed in the drunkenness of passion: the landscape of the body . . . . These landscapes are traversed by paths which lead sexuality into the world of the inorganic. Fashion itself is only another medium enticing it still more deeply into the universe of matter.

Fashion stands in opposition to the organic. It couples the living body to the inorganic world. To the living, it defends the rights of the corpse. The fetishism that succumbs to the sex appeal of the inorganic is its vital nerve. The cult of the commodity presses such fetishism into its service.

The Arcades Project

The poets were onto it long before Freud,
The love-death thing, the *Liebestod* conceit.
From Petrarch down they relished bitter-sweet
Ideas of love that told us 'once enjoyed,
Those pleasures, they remind us of the void
That lies in wait, or how our thought to cheat
Death's cold embrace through love's rekindling heat
Must end with vital spirits self-destroyed'.
They all – Villon to Shakespeare, Lovelace, Donne,
Marvell and later poets in that line –
Turned 'die' or 'little death' into a pun-
Like quip, a racy catchword to combine
Remembered or imagined joys with un-
Unabashed reminders of the death's-head sign.

Freud took it further, stressed how close the tie
Of love and death, and told us – in 'Beyond
The Pleasure-Principle' – just how that bond
Of drives or psychic forces that must lie,
You'd think, at opposite extremes may tie
Our logic up in knots because, *au fond*,
Those primal drives in no way correspond
To ego's protest that the one word, 'die,'
Not serve for both. Think rather, he advised,
How closely they're entwined, the primal deed

Of life by lovestruck poets duly prized
Above all others, and the fate decreed
For living flesh by what – as he surmised –
Prepared it for the worms it soon must feed.

And further still he drove it, that idea
So alien to the eudaimonic sense
Of life and love that calls in self-defence
Whatever back-up from the ego-sphere
May give it some short-lived distractive steer
Around the ego-censored truth: that whence
We came, shall we return; that 'the expense
Of spirit' is 'a waste of shame,' though we're
Too self-deceived to know. The death-drive haunts
Our love-lives, sounds uncannily in each
Last gasp of passion stilled, and duly taunts
Those who'd take lightly what it has to teach
With the decisive mortal denouements
That put immortal pleasures out of reach.

For even while the lover lives and burns
With passion yet unslaked, that fierce desire
Pervades their flesh with a consuming fire
That frets it to the bone and thus returns
It sooner to the state for which it yearns,
That inorganic state where pores transpire
Not with the moisture that love's heats require
But with the damp that funerary urns
Can't long keep in or out. That's why the passion
For other things, like shifting styles of dress,
May strike the viewer as dead matter's ration
Of hybrid substitutes that coalesce
With living flesh until the latest fashion
Becomes the last for earth to repossess.

That sexuality's our strongest clue
To thanatos and its incessant drive
For death, oblivion, all that man alive
So often seeks to place beneath taboo –
That's Freud's dark tale, and one that we might do

Well sometimes to recall, not further strive
Against its strict refusal to deprive
Our bliss-deluded kind of what's their true
Since fleshly lot in life. Then we might trace
Those paths by which the death-drive came to leave
Its imprint everywhere in psychic space,
Determine in advance what we conceive
As 'life' and 'death,' and so ensure we base
Life-choices on a death-drive none should grieve.

The Serpent's Trail

But where the human form withdraws from photography, there for
the first time display value gets the better of cultic value. And it is
having set the scene for this process to occur that gives Atget, the
man who captured so many deserted Parisian streets around 1900,
his incomparable significance. Quite rightly it has been said of him
that he recorded those streets like crime scenes. A crime scene, too, is
deserted. Atget snaps clues. With Atget, photographs become exhibits
in the trial that is history.

> 'The Work of Art in the Age of
> Mechanical Reproduction'

To articulate the past historically does not mean to recognize it 'the
way it really was' (Ranke). It means to seize hold of a memory as it
flashes up at a moment of danger. Historical materialism wishes to
retain that image of the past which unexpectedly appears to man
singled out by history at a moment of danger.

> 'Theses on the Philosophy of History'

The trail of the human serpent is thus over everything.

> William James, 'What Pragmatism Means'

1

'The human interest' – don't allow that phrase,
So tired, debased, and barnacled with all
The detritus of bourgeois works and days,
To have you think the only photo-call
Worth turning up for's one that shows in small
And yet, somehow, in depth what best conveys
Our own, or anyone's, especial traits,
The marks of weal and woe, hopes low and high,
The times of peace hard-won, the sudden squall,
Life-crises, scenes to gladden or appal,
And every token, to the camera's eye,
Of what we kindred souls should know them by.

2

Don't let it take you in, that pantomime
Of 'inner life' that bids you junk the whole
Idea of things, like inner-city crime,
Or poverty, or millions on the dole,
Or civil strife, by which your talk of 'soul,'
That bourgeois throwback to a monkish time,
Might lose its old, consolatory chime
And tell you: look within and all you find
Is stage-machinery in his control,
That new director who's assumed the role
Of author, lead, and dramaturg combined,
Plus scene-shift duties as and when assigned.

3

For it's just when that 'inner life' retreats,
When 'human interest' interests nobody,
And the rogue camera hits the roguish streets –
That's when photography can claim to be,
'Authentically,' perhaps, the truest key
To what transpires on those forbidden beats
Where at first light unfinished business greets
The roving camera-man who has us shed
Whatever lingering illusions we
Might have about last-ditch humanity
And, through his graphic witness, put to bed
Those myths the bourgeois portrait-painters fed.

4

He knows, that street-wise shutterbug surely knows,
That what's gone missing since the burghers sat
For brush-poised sycophants and struck their pose
Of nonchalant fake disinterest (Kant my hat!)
Is all that once defined the habitat
They both enjoyed their place in, whether those
Who paid or those who painted, since their shows
Of cross-class amity might thus display,
Improbably, how both were aiming at
An inner essence and, along with that,

The marks of social standing that convey:
'My wealth, my art, my soul – what's more to say?'.

5

His art shows all: the boulevards, the run-
Down precincts, *quartiers*, mansions gone to seed,
The bad-lands, good-lands, areas just begun
On the long slide, though – should his travels lead,
Perchance, to some eventual, snap-decreed
Odd bit of 'human interest' – it has none
Of that fake inner life on which were spun
So many fantasies, so many love-
Or fear-engendered tales to serve the need
For soulmates good or bad with whom to feed
The endless craving that, push come to shove,
You'll have their sort to rank yourself above.

6

So ask yourself: when human life withdraws,
In Atget's snapshots, from the hollow sphere
Whose cleft halves cling against the dread that gnaws
At their fond dream of union, should we fear
His further pushing-back of the frontier
Between the human soul, that near-lost cause,
And all that presses on it without pause,
Or should we rather think this helps reveal,
By just that shrewd technique, the clues that we're
So keen to have ourselves and others steer
Well clear of, yet in whose discovery he'll
Show truths less soul-sustaining but more real?

7

Think how those *banlieues*, zones of conflict, no-
Go areas, red-light districts, or the mean-
Street purlieus where the violence boils below
The heat-cracked sidewalks loom up like the scene
Of an atrocious crime that's somehow been
So deftly covered up that even Poe
Would stretch things somewhat to have Dupin know,

By swift inspection, what had brought about
The eerie sense of that which vanished clean
Away yet left enough for us to glean
Some sense of clues that might, with luck, bear out
A shrewd conjecture now placed beyond doubt.

8

It's the same faith, I'd venture, that impelled
The lens-sleuth Atget to pursue those shots
Which, read aright, so accurately spelled
The message out for anyone who plots
The curve, the narrowing range of viewer-slots
For devotees of inner life who held
A sagging fallback line. Then they rebelled,
Like Atget's bourgeois critic-foes, against
His sharp-eyed joining of the psychic dots
That showed, with undeceiving rigour, what's
Made life so hard for those who sought a fenced-
Off place for soul and went unrecompensed.

9

Where but in history can we make trial
Of their unwilling witness to the fate
Of inner life, the ones whose long denial
Of every latest threat to nihilate
Its remnant traces recognised their state
And turned for guidance to the growing pile
Of press-reports and photographs on file
That show, now unmistakably, how far
And fast it's climbed, the soul's attrition-rate,
Until the surest means to calibrate
Time's passage is deciphering where we are,
Historically, as Atget shifts the bar.

10

One comfort: as it shifts, so we perceive
How, subject-pole to object-pole, its course
Requires we turn materialist and leave
Behind those soul-imaginings, the source –

As now we recognise – of every force
That drives us backward, has us vainly cleave
To other-worldly goods, and so achieve
No more in this – our one and only world –
Than, yet again, the pitiless divorce
That Plato draws between the docile horse
Of soulful wisdom and the chariot hurled
About by one with instinct's flag unfurled.

11

For now it's history as viewed by Klee's
Distraught *rücksichtlich* Angel that may yield
Perspectives aptly fashioned for the gaze
Of us late-comers to the battlefield
Of warring memories. What's then revealed,
At least to minds sufficiently in phase,
Is the oft-damped yet oft-resurgent blaze
That shines a revelatory new light –
Though I'd prefer to say 'a light concealed
By the weak messianic gift to shield
Its unprepared beholders' – on the night
Of hopes forlorn till now kept out of sight.

12

Call 'history' the precinct long laid waste
By victor-souls where hope may yet revive,
Though intermittently, and where the taste
Of noble spirits crushed will have us strive
More zealously to see the hour arrive
When he, Klee's Angel, radiant, future-faced,
Unfolds his shining pinions now storm-braced
To ride the air, thick streaming with the smashed-
Up hope-invested fragments of a live
Though unachieved potential that may drive
Him onward, tempest-borne and debris-lashed,
To seize his chance when next the signal's flashed.

Halos and *Haeccitas* (Duns Scotus, Agamben, Benjamin)

In *The Coming Community* . . . [Giorgio] Agamben recounts a Jewish parable about the world to come in which 'everything will be as it is now, just a little different'. Instead of a colossal destruction followed by massive rebuilding, the Day of Judgment involves an almost imperceptible displacement of the present order of things. This small difference reminds Agamben of Aquinas's approach to halos, which do not alter in any essential way the blessed bodies they surround.

David Kishik, 'I Can See Your Halo'

Perhaps one of those [angels] who, according to the Talmud, are at each moment created anew in countless throngs, and who, once they have raised their voices before God, cease and pass into nothingness. Lamenting, chastising, rejoicing?

Benjamin, *Reflections*

Note: 'the subtle Doctor' = Duns Scotus; 'Doctor Angelicus' = St. Thomas Aquinas

1

Let each have their own halo, so he thought,
The Subtle Doctor, he who found a way
To grant all body-souls the bliss they sought.
Doctor Angelicus saw fit to say
That halos were, in general, OK,
Not plainly nor doctrinally absurd,
Though he, like Benjamin, chose to convey
This counsel in the textual form preferred
By one with no great zeal to spread the word.

The trouble with that glorious array
Of shining headbands was the point that naught
Was needed, or allowed, to somehow play
The added-value role of that which brought
One more perfection to the sum that ought,
By right, t'have shown the scholars how they erred

Since adding it would mean the sum fell short,
Till then, of such perfection as conferred
The halo like a deficit incurred.

2

Duns Scotus, kindlier-hearted, begged he might
Just save appearances could he but tweak
His master's metaphysics and put right
This strange anomaly that some would seek
To use for leverage on that single weak,
Albeit load-bearing point. Could they but see
Those halos as what made each one unique,
Each soul embodied, body heavenly,
They'd once more find good cause to bend the knee.

Perceive the *haeccitas*, the nth degree
Of this-ness, hallmark of the heteroclite,
The inscape, instress, utmost quiddity
Of every being, and you'll bring to light –
To fullest radiance – what lay out of sight
So long as we viewed everything oblique,
Let custom veil what flashed up pure and bright,
And so stayed blind to all in each physique
That bore the halo's singular mystique.

3

It's Russell's paradox, and Gödel's too,
The set or axiom one must include
To make the scheme complete but which will do,
Once counted in, such mischiefs as accrued
To mathematics once those thinkers skewed
Its onward path from Hilbert's sanguine list
Of coming breakthroughs to a multitude
Of looming undecidables that missed
The dateline for each next 'eureka' tryst.

What room for halos when they must consist
In some transcendent state arrived at through
The sum of all perfections, yet exist

Not as an essence superadded to
That self-sufficient sum but as their due,
Their 'singular completion' now construed
By way of its potential to imbue
Each with the radiance that must else elude
Our senses when dispassionately viewed?

4

What relevance to us, you'll say, what kind
Of lesson's there for us in this debate
Between old schoolmen, we who've left behind
Such arcane matters that can scarcely rate
A moment's thought from those who'd dedicate
Their time to serious things? Yet, quite aside
From Russell, Gödel and the growing spate
Of formal teasers, there's this point that I'd
Best put to you, much closer home applied.

Call 'halo' that which lovers co-create
In special moments, those they take as guide
When thinking to retrieve, revive, postdate,
Or summon what such radiant scenes provide
By way of showing what the rest may hide
Through constantly contriving to remind
Them of the Lethean, halo-dimming slide
From such rare heights to life-scenes where they find
Love's lineaments less angelically outlined.

5

Think too of Hopkins, he whose every phrase
Of keen-eared metric counterpoint or keen-
Eyed metaphor brings to our mental gaze,
With Scotus' blessing, all that's to be seen
In face and figure till they supervene,
Those halos, and, sans supplement, complete
What always and already must have been,
By strict Aquinan diktat, in receipt
Of all perfections where they singly meet.

And then there's Benjamin, shrewd exegete
Of arcane texts, discoverer of ways
To find hope's glimmer in each past defeat,
And chronicler whose cryptic text conveys
How best to thread the allegoric maze
Of meanings glimpsed, lost sight of, caught between
Redemption's dawn and history's delays,
A chastened visionary alert to glean
Life-signs from barbarism's Soylent Green.

Not his the Saul-to-Paul or Damascene
Conversion, nor the mystic's zeal to greet
Some total rupture with that old routine
Of brute injustice destined to repeat
Itself so long as every balance-sheet
Reads 'Us and Them'. Rather, he'll paraphrase,
Interpret, annotate, close-read, and treat
The texts of history, like those *Trauerspiel* plays,
As hieroglyphs of human works and days.

6

No halos, no brave victories, nothing so
Assured of future progress as to buy
Back into that old slaughter-pile and go
Triumphantly along with each new lie
The conquerors tell to drown the victim's cry,
Re-write the story, give another spin
To all those epic tales of do or die,
And thereby show once more what Benjamin
Reveals in every myth of origin.

And yet, when once we cease to revel in
Great deeds and rather set ourselves to show
What horrors long repressed still underpin
The victory-parades, then we can know,
At just those flashed-up instants when the flow
Of homogeneous time stops dead, just why
Our inner Hegel's somehow forced to slow,
Then halt his onward passage to a high
Point only history's butchers occupy.

It's here the medievalist may descry
A shrewd redemptive strategy akin
To that which let his subtle mind apply
Its (let's not kid ourselves) distinctly thin
Or wire-drawn argument. If halos win
Acceptance it's because they may bestow
The kind of radiance Scotus deems no sin
Since it, like Benjamin's, extends the glow
Of *haeccitas* to beings here below.

7

Be clear: nowhere but in the earthly hell
Of secular history can that slim hope,
That glint of halos trashed, remain to tell
The fractured narrative or offer scope
For its weak messianic power to trope
The spoils of conquest and discover where
In that parade dim figures interlope
To image forth what's hidden in the *clair-*
Obscur cast on them by the victor's glare.

Gentlest of heresies, and one they'd cope
With easily enough, the halo fell
In place for churchmen like an isotope
Of faith's own element, or the pell-mell
Of history whose onrush leaves the shell-
Shocked Angel wings spread, pinioned, treading air,
And gazing back at the storm-driven swell,
Yet bearing forward as if prefigured there,
Though fleetingly, hope's elemental share.

Benjamin's Kafka: Failure as Destiny

(with excursion on Beckett)

> To do justice to the figure of Kafka in its purity and peculiar beauty one must never lose sight of one thing; it is the purity and beauty of failure . . . . One is tempted to say: once he was certain of eventual failure, everything worked out for him *en route* as in a dream.

> Even if Kafka did not pray – and this we do not know – he still possessed in the highest degree what Malebranche called 'the natural prayer of the soul': attentiveness. And in this attentiveness he included all living creatures, as saints include them in their prayers.

> Franz Kafka, in *Illuminations*

> All as of old. Nothing else ever. Ever tried. Ever failed. No matter. Try again. Fail again. Fail better.

> Samuel Beckett, *Worstward Ho*

1

The Beckett line: fail better next time, fail
The more successfully because success
At failing must on no account entail
Some notion that the failure matters less,
Or needn't count as such, since you possess
A decent claim to do what failures do
But a bit better, as if chance should bless
Your previous upsets with, at last, a few
Small happy outcomes, just to see you through.

Still there's a sense that failure seems to suit
The Beckett view of things so well, or play
Out in such dire predicaments *en route*
To every woeful close, that one might say
Success for him, as for his whole array
Of dead-end failures, fictive or on-stage,
Was measured by just how completely they
Fulfilled their obligation to assuage
His drive to nihilate them, page by page.

2

But then there's Kafka, he whom we should hail
Mistakenly – so Benjamín would stress –
If we presume to place him on a scale
Where failure finds its readiest redress
Through just such willingness to acquiesce,
Like Beckett's devotees, in every cue
For terminal despair that might impress
The existentialists yet stoop to woo
The groundlings with a comic twist or two.

No call for tragic sigh or comic hoot
With Kafka, nothing but the *dieu caché*
Of dull routine, hopes lost, lives destitute,
Shades of death's prison-house for Josef K,
Or Gregor Samsa faced at break of day
With waving insect-legs that must presage,
By all the rules of this grim cabaret,
That his ill chance will soon provoke the rage
Of folk reliant on his weekly wage.

3

What lay the other side of flat despair
Was Benjamin's 'weak messianic' theme,
With Kafka's – strange to say – the proof-texts where
He found them both prefigured, the regime
Of past afflictions and the shattered dream
Whose storm-tossed fragments signify some pure
If fabled source-point whose residual gleam
May yet outshine the perilous allure
Of futures booked or prospects premature.

Still Kafka warns: no last hopes to redeem
Save those invested in the strength to bear
Whatever lethal jetsam piles upstream
Or one last taunt the Doorman may prepare
To greet the Countryman who's waited there
A lifetime, held 'before the law' whose sure
If sluggard process labours to ensnare

The supplicant pre-sentenced to endure
Its insolence with door now locked secure.

How then should we refuse the title 'prayer'
To the long vigil that made up his tour
Of baffled watchfulness, his own lost share
In every chance his characters abjure
To take fresh heart or, likelier, inure
Themselves conjointly to the relay-team
Of doorkeepers whose brute imprimatur
Is all they warrant in their author's scheme
To fail-mark failure's failure-proof extreme.

Art, Aura and Politics

Even the most perfect reproduction of a work of art is lacking in one element: its presence in time and space, its unique existence at the place where it happens to be.

At the instant the criterion of authenticity ceases to be applicable to artistic production, the total function of art is reversed. Instead of being based on ritual, it begins to be based on another practice – politics.

To perceive the aura of an object we look at means to invest it with the ability to look at us in return.

'The Work of Art in the Age of
Mechanical Reproduction'

[T]he spoils are carried along in the procession. They are called cultural treasures, and a historical materialist views them with cautious detachment.

'Theses on the Philosophy of History'

1

What marks the artwork is its here-and-now.
There's one place only where the work must be.
No reproduction fills that time and space.

The replicas are splendid, let's allow;
They've gone up-market, that we can agree.
Good for the boardroom wall, in any case.

And let's not make 'the work' our sacred cow,
The object of some crass art-dealer's spree
Or holy grail for culture-snobs to chase.

Else we'll just join the legions of high-brow
But low-grade art investors who can see
No values save those of the market-place.

It's that unique location tells us how
To let the work claim authenticity
And so avoid technology's embrace.

Let something of that aura still endow
Its sole original, remain the key
To why we feel: *that's it*, the work we face.

For else the flood of replicas will wow
The crowds but leave the replicator free
To fool the unsuspecting populace.

2

And yet, and yet . . . those replicas begin,
With new technology, to fool the eye
Of all but the most practised connoisseur.

And think: if they're so quickly taken in,
Should we despise the goods they're flummoxed by?
At least those hard distinctions start to blur.

Too soon we jump to talk of origin,
Of aura, masterwork, and suchlike high-
Art terms got up precisely to confer

On those originals a value-spin
That has them all, routinely, a far cry
From replicas that fool the amateur.

Then there's Brecht's point: don't trap the arts within
The same old art-snob circle where small-fry
Or working-class art-lovers mustn't stir

Things up by messing with the firing-pin
Of their art-canon where the great works lie
Close-guarded lest such upsets should occur.

Much better get them out there, let them win
New viewers, readers, listeners who'll try
Their strength against the cultural powers that were.

3

Like it or not, Bert says, we're living through
An epoch when there's scarcely any sphere
Of life untouched by replication's sway.

Why cling to aura's dwindling residue
When techno-culture makes the message clear:
What if you art-elites have had your day?

Through replication art deprives the few
Of their ancestral right to commandeer
The culture-heights and always have their say

On who's to gain, who loses, who's to screw
The culture-hungry workers, and whose rear-
Guard tastes are just the price those workers pay.

It's replication moves them up the queue,
Puts string quartets on disc so folk can hear
Them any time, presents a Shakespeare play

On radio, or brings to public view
(Joe Public, not the bourgeois upper tier)
The Titians, Rembrandts, plus the odd Monet.

All to the good, he says, and rightly: who
Could link hands with the culture-snobs who sneer
At any good things put the workers' way?

4

And yet . . . 'good things'? Often enough it's those
'Great works' of ours, the favoured props and stays
Of my, and Bertolt's, and (for let's not beat

About the bush) Karl Marx's sort who chose
High Culture's chequered flag as one to raise
On the long march to capital's defeat.

That washing's what we take in, and it shows:
No learned mention dropped, no turn of phrase,
No classic line or stanza we repeat

But tells the others, be they friends or foes,
That if it's 'bourgeois values' this betrays
We've not let down our comrades on the street.

I tend to stress this point because it goes
Hard with me when I think of how it plays
With them, the hard-core activists I meet,

Who say I'd do much better to disclose
How those 'great works' with laurel, oak and bays
Are stuff dreamt up to keep the boss-class sweet

And not the stuff it takes to ward off blows
From truncheons, strive to douse the *Reichstag*-blaze,
Or come back fighting after each retreat.

5

Too well I know the hideous truths that hide
Their blood-stained history as much behind
The paintings, poems, novels, string quartets

As under the processions sanctified
By Church and State to keep us well in mind
Of how they'd act on suchlike festive threats.

Show me your great works laid out side-by-side,
The finest products of the most refined
Or visionary spirits, and their debts

To conquest, war, oppression, genocide
And sheer barbarities of every kind
Will strike a note that no one soon forgets

Who's known, like me, the terrors that can ride
On regime-change or treaties newly signed
Which bring swift closure of the border-nets.

That art thrives on injustice – truth denied
By gentler souls, though not by those inclined
To ask on whose far realms the sun ne'er sets.

Artworks adorn the juggernauts of pride
In empire as if purposely designed
To grace the slaughter with choice epithets.

6

For me, I scarcely hope to reconcile
The voice in me that counsels 'never share
Those secondary spoils that lend their name

As "masterworks" to culture's growing pile
Of corpses', and the voice that bids me bear
Due witness to that catalogue of shame,

Bad faith and conqueror-worship even while
I strive to honour art's ongoing share
In those redemptive powers it yet might claim.

We scholars, too, before we close the file
On all our tyrant-coddling, head-in-air
Political false steps, and playing-tame

With monsters, can declare we've borne the trial
Of history in ways fit to compare
With Roland's, he who to the dark tower came.

And should those works or texts chance to beguile
Our patient *studium* with the *punctum* they're
Yet holding in reserve, then who's to blame

The aura-lovers, those whose logophile
Vocation or addiction shows their care
For rules not those of any victors' game.

For Asja Lacis

In a love affair, most seek an eternal homeland. Others, but very few, eternal voyaging. These latter are melancholics, for whom contact with mother earth is to be shunned. They seek the person who will keep far from them the homeland's sadness. To that person, they remain faithful.

The only way of knowing a person is to love them without hope.

The idea that happiness could have a share in beauty would be too much of a good thing.

One-Way Street and Other Writings

1

'True to thee in my fashion,' so he wrote;
Don't rank me with that English decadent!
True, he half-struck the melancholic note:
The voyaging, the *nostos*-swerving quest.
'True to thee in my fashion,' so he wrote,
And maybe sought her likeness as he went,
Encountering other women, seeking rest
Yet ever restless, 'home' the asymptote
He'd oftentimes strike out for once he'd spent
Too long away, but then head further West.
'True to thee in my fashion,' so he wrote.
Don't rank me with that English decadent!
The voyaging, the *nostos*-swerving quest.

2

I loved you, Asja, loved no-one but you.
God knows it's exile drove me land to land.
That poet, Dowson, 1890s crew –
Their melancholy's just an aesthete's pose.
I loved you, Asja, loved no-one but you.
To Latvia, Moscow, Berlin – nothing planned
Except to seek you, go where Asja goes.
And then, when news came of the Hitler coup
And borders closed to me on every hand,

Yours was the first, best dwelling-place I chose.
I loved you, Asja, loved no-one but you.
God knows it's exile drove me land to land.
Their melancholy's just an aesthete's' pose.

3

So closely our two lives, thoughts, fates entwined!
You, comrade, knocked the bourgeois out of me,
Told me 'read Marx,' gave lessons of the kind
It took to bring this scholar back to earth.
So closely our two lives, thoughts, fates entwined!
You, with Bert Brecht, taught me the abc
Of communist theatre, showed the worth
Of workers' education, turned my mind
To dialectics as the only key
To all that might yet bring new times, new birth.
So closely our two lives, thoughts, fates entwined!
You, comrade, knocked the bourgeois out of me.
Took you to bring this scholar back to earth.

4

Lessons in love were not the least you taught.
Why make a passion shared one's highest aim?
No fixed or charted star, the love I sought;
Solace, like refuge, always far to seek.
Lessons in love were not the least you taught.
From sundry lands your wandering call-sign came,
From lands remote with messages oblique:
A letting-go, the change in me you wrought.
Yet still I loved, still sought you just the same,
Though now of politics, not love, we'd speak.
Lessons in love were not the least you taught.
Why make a passion shared one's highest aim?
Solace, like refuge, always far to seek.

5

We lived together, once, but you moved on.
My flights to exile, yours to tasks unknown.
How fortune-crossed, our guiltless liaison!
Your tasks cast mine in an unflattering light.

We lived together, once, but you moved on,
I in my shifting, shiftless scholar-zone,
You teaching, acting, putting kids' lives right.
Our lives unwound like chant and antiphon,
Or lines cross-keyed to each successive tone.
What odds, what threats, what fears you had to fight!
We lived together, once, but you moved on.
My flights to exile, yours to tasks unknown.
Your tasks cast mine in an unflattering light.

6

Heimat: to me it means unending loss,
My homes-from-home mere variants on the theme.
Let others risk their necks to gather moss.
Dasein, begone from Heidegger's domain!
Heimat: to me it means unending loss.
You, Asja, spurned the groves of academe,
Found no such refuge from a teeming brain,
And turned to drama as your active gloss,
A Brechtian one, on what my scholar's dream
Dictates be done through readings more arcane.
Heimat: to me it means unending loss,
My homes-from-home mere variants on the theme.
Dasein, begone from Heidegger's domain!

7

Fatherland, mother-earth: how think to choose?
No dwelling but may trap the hunted soul.
Who'd not turn constant exile in my shoes?
You've your theatre, Marx, the rebel's fire!
Fatherland, mother-earth: how think to choose?
One choice at least for you: the choice of role,
Whether close-matched to your express desire,
Like Brecht's cut-back 'Good Woman' ('scenes to lose,'
You told him!), or because the times that stole
My home gave all the stage-room you'd require.
Fatherland, mother-earth: how think to choose?
No dwelling but may trap the hunted soul.
You've your theatre, Marx, the rebel's fire!

8

We melancholics count what joys we've had.
Though fugitive, you were the chief of mine.
Snatched moments must suffice when times are bad.
You, self-propelled, made good my exile state.
We melancholics count what joys we've had.
I know you found them strange and byzantine,
Those texts I strove to read, parse, annotate,
And – yes – deploy in ways that, you were glad
To note, gave real-world, extra-textual spine
To revolution, could we but translate.
We melancholics count what joys we've had.
Though fugitive, you were the chief of mine.
You, self-propelled, made good my exile state.

9

'To the loved one far absent' – what more apt?
How else should wandering *Sehnsucht* stay its fears?
Not, to be sure, by *Heimkehr* safely mapped!
Whereabouts roughly known, but not for long.
'To the loved one far absent' – what more apt?
The words and music haunted me for years,
Brought thoughts of you to mind in every song
Of that Beethoven cycle, and thus tapped
Into both my old terror of frontiers
And sense of how your crossings made me strong.
'To the loved one far absent' – what more apt?
How else should wandering *Sehnsucht* stay its fears?
Whereabouts roughly known, but not for long.

10

No goal for you, 'eternal voyaging'.
'Elsewhere' meant things to do when you upped sticks.
To you, my 'elsewhere' had a dreamer's ring.
Forget the Kibbutz, we've a world to win!
No goal for you, 'eternal voyaging'.
Always your schedule: next stop politics!
Such forking paths for souls so close akin;
Your thoughts took timely flight while mine took wing.

You got your tips from comrades, Bolsheviks,
And Brecht while I . . . . but, dearest, how begin?
No goal for you, 'eternal voyaging'.
'Elsewhere' meant things to do when you upped sticks.
Forget the Kibbutz, we've a world to win!

11

Think of that piece that Brecht and Eisler did,
That song about the little radio-set
The exile carried off with him and hid.
Always I yearned to catch the day's home news –
Think of that song that Brecht and Eisler did.
He tuned in, dawn and dusk, to hear things get
More desperate day by day while you, the muse
Of all those early writings, had me bid
You serve as my fixed compass-point and let
My arm track home at last to Syracuse.
Think of that piece that Brecht and Eisler did,
That song about the little radio-set.
Always I yearned to catch the day's home news.

Nunc Stans: Monad and Messiah

A historical materialist approaches a historical subject only where he encounters it as a monad. In this structure he recognizes the sign of a Messianic cessation of happening, or, put differently, a revolutionary chance in the fight for the oppressed past.

The danger affects both the content of the tradition and its receivers. The same threat hangs over both: that of becoming a tool of the ruling classes. In every era the attempt must be made anew to wrest tradition away from a conformism that is about to overpower it.

'Theses on the Philosophy of History'

1

That's when it dawns, in that split second when
The hope-forlorn historian whose
Life-giving element
Is time itself must somehow choose.
First choice: lay down that hope-annulling pen
Of yours, select some other muse
Than Clio, and present
Your readers with emollient views
More apt to draw at least a quiet 'amen'
From folk with so few hopes to lose,
And those – like yours – long spent
In seeking witness that accrues,
Albeit in fits and starts, to the old yen
For history that still pursues
The onward course that lent
Their tale a shape one might excuse
For smoothing out the upsets now and then.

2

Then second choice: conceive that stock idea
Of history as the way things go
Along time's placid stream
As if in a continuous flow
That may, on rare occasions, buck and veer

Through turbulence – conceive it so,
And you'll join the regime
Of smoothers-out who aim to show,
As liberals early on in their career,
How small tweaks to the status quo
Should be the chronicler's theme,
Not major shake-ups such as throw
The whole progress-machinery out of gear
('All those failed revolutions, no?'),
But who most often seem
To end up airing views that grow
More fascist-sounding latter year to year.

3

The metaphysician Leibniz thought to see,
In his idealist monads, all
He needed to imbue
The real with wherewithal
To vindicate its rationality
So naught contingent might befall
Their occupants or do
The kinds of mischief to appal
Those, like himself, whose God would guarantee
Events in each hermetic ball
To carry on with due
Regard to the great mirror-hall
Of trans-monadic intercourse, the key –
He thought – to having nothing fall
Outside the overview
Of Him who had benign last call
In knowing just what can and cannot be.

4

Mere metaphysics, empty talk, you'll say,
And I'd not cavil with you there,
But none the less insist
That Leibniz has some truths to share
With those for whom idealist thought might play
Not just the role of more hot air

Or intellectual grist
To bourgeois mills but rather bear,
Though in a strange, oblique, contorted way,
Due witness to what can, with care,
Take a materialist
Inflection, show how far they err,
The Leibniz scholars who've long failed to pay
This aspect of his thought a fair
Traversal and so missed
What it reveals to those who dare
Draw out material truths it might convey.

5

So, truth the first: that history's not one
Continuous, long, unfolding line
Of happenings that make
Sufficient sense beneath the sign
Of some grand narrative or story spun
Either to polish up the shine
On 'progress' or to take
It off by framing tales to spline
Choice instances of how, 'in the long run,'
Events and human faults combine
To reassert the stake
Of 'realism,' 'commonsense,' 'divine
Displeasure,' or 'naught new under the sun,'
And – so conservatives opine –
Discredit those who fake
Such upbeat yarns (lest their cloud nine
Of sundry downbeat variants be outdone!).

6

And truth the second: simply break the spell
Of that Teutonic gospel spread,
For reasons of their own,
By Ranke and the mighty dead
Of German historiography who tell
A tale whose upshot may be said
To haunt the danger-zone

Where over-zealous souls are led,
By factual-seeming narratives, to dwell
On what's conveyed by what they've read,
Or what they've only known
As way-points strung along a thread
Whose end-point's often one more heaven-turned-hell.
Thus wise historians fear to tread
A *meta hodos* prone
To consummations we should dread
When once we've learned their cautious lesson well.

7

That's why the humble chronicler can aid
The cause of justice (hence the cause
Of revolution) by
Eschewing any talk of 'laws'
In history, even laws expressly made
To fit the odd exception-clause,
And waiting to descry,
Perhaps in some arhythmic pause
Of actions and events, the call once laid
To rest (no trumpets, no applause!)
But now at last raised high
In the *nunc stans* that swiftly draws
That chronicler to seek out just what stayed
Her mental gaze and told her 'Yours,
This hope left high and dry
By history which now implores
You, its sole bearer, not to let it fade'.

8

God knows we've no use for a new Messiah!
The false ones still pop up and bring
More mockery, or start
New wars although they always sing
Of peace, or promise you your heart's desire,
Then clear off and leave everything
Either an applecart
Upturned or faith to which you cling

Like Brecht's poor Mother Courage, worth her hire
In war-dead sons and hopes. No king,
No 'son of God,' no part
In all that abject grovelling
Before whichever monarch, Pope, or squire
Besought it as of right. Unstring
The twanging harps, take heart,
And say: no victor-god can spring
Such messianic hopes as we require!

9

The weak messiah's 'weak' just in so far
As he or she declines a place
In any victor's train,
Pours scorn on talk of 'master-race,'
Or 'race' *tout court*, or covert colour-bar,
Or thinly-veiled attempt to base
Class-violence on a strain
Of victor-thought that bears the trace,
In word or deed, of that which might well jar
With their own views could they but face
How much against the grain
It goes with them, that forced embrace
Of values and beliefs whose guiding star
Shines in a constellated space
So far from home terrain
That such weak-messianic grace
Is all that might yet heal the culture-scar.

Misery and Beauty: Parables

Kafka's real genius was that he tried something entirely new: he sacrificed truth for the sake of clinging to its transmissibility . . . . Kafka's writings are by their nature parables. But it is their misery and their beauty that they had to become more than parables . . . . Though apparently reduced to submission, they unexpectedly raise a mighty paw against it.

'Reflections on Kafka'

'The misery and the beauty': so I wrote
To Scholem in regard to Kafka's way
With parables, his constant need to stray
Beyond the parabolic asymptote
Where lesser writers heed the warning note:
'Seek not by mere transmittance to convey
Such truths as you must strive to hold at bay
Lest they turn out a mix of anecdote,
Life-guide, and moral tale'. Yet those who keep
That caution well in mind are justly held
His, Kafka's, wise but lesser brethren whose
Restraint in never going dark and deep
Nor heaven-high abjured that risk yet spelled
It out: small thanks for nothing much to lose!

'Truth or transmissibility': don't take
The critics' word for it, their standard line
On Kafka's parables that would assign
Deep truths or timeless verities – 'Thus spake
The riddling sage!' – yet see it prove deep fake
By seeking new profundities to mine
And then – what shows the process asinine –
Returning with some message fit to make
Poor Kafka laugh or squirm. Those words 'transmit,'
'Transmissible' – they have a tale to tell,
A story, almost parable, that goes
Deft ways around to show how surely it
Must miss the mark if commentators dwell
On truths they're fully licenced to disclose.

Always one step ahead, that's Kafka's great
Though strangely self-defeating trick to let
Us in on it, the way that those dead-set
On truth-as-revelation have to skate
Across the gaps and trip-wires that dictate,
For readers not so over-keen to get
The point, a sojourn in the never-yet
Of parabolic sense where meanings wait
On truths as yet unvouched. So much we know,
We Kafka-trained old lags, but may detect
The leopard-spores already there within
The temple, evidence enough to show
His touch, however light, poised to direct
Our reading once the sacraments begin.

It's Kafka's oblique tribute to the role
Of story-teller, that which bids him raise
A paw to see that his communiqués
Not totally submit to the control
Of parable and so endure the toll
On native gift and talent that he pays
Who, unlike Kafka, readily obeys
The tacit rule: make 'code unknown' the whole
Of your decoder's kit. Not so with him,
Franz Kafka, great parabolist of these
Our secular times whose texts require such care
Of readers – not the sort you'd want to skim! –
Yet who, like Christ, takes measures to appease
The yen for revelation lurking there.

Toys and Play

We must not forget that the most enduring modifications in toys are never the work of adults, whether educators, manufacturers or writers, but are the result of children at play.

For who gives the child his toys if not adults? And even if he retains a certain power to accept or reject them, a not insignificant proportion of the oldest toys (balls, hoops, tops, kites) are in a certain sense imposed on him as cult-implements that become toys only afterwards, partly through the child's powers of imagination.

The process of emancipating the toy begins. The more industrialization penetrates, the more decisively it eludes the control of the family and becomes increasingly alien to children and also to parents.

One-Way Street and Other Writings

Give the toy-makers, market-watchers, crews
Of watchful adults, teachers, salesmen-squads,
And so forth – give them time and what's the odds
That, just a century on, you might well choose
To date that first pronouncement, maybe lose
The 'never,' and acknowledge how the gods
Of industry and finance make the mods
And tweaks while it's the ad-hooked kid who screws
The pre-fab bits together. 'Play' indeed,
Play of a kind, but look for any sign
Of creativity, inventiveness,
Or technical resource and you'll concede
That making sure the bits and bobs align
'As shown' must signify: regress, regress!

Call me a Luddite, sentimentalist,
Or harker-back to my own childhood days
When 'things were so much simpler,' and I'll raise
No great objection save to say you've missed
My point: that kids can make a decent fist
Still, in our age, of doing things in ways
Much cleverer, more rewarding than when play's
Become just following plans that pre-exist
And pre-require each plug-in. How ignore

The larger context here, the Fordist-style
Production-line, the task that alienates
The worker from his work, the endless chore
That puts an end to all that's versatile,
Free-thinking, innovative – suspect traits!

We thinkers, too, must sense the growing threat
When, grown-up children, we assemble thoughts,
Words, idea-constellations, and all sorts
Of hybrid artefact in forms as yet
Untried, hence with no standard to be met
Or plan provided, no kit-builder 'oughts'
That treat inventiveness as school-reports
Treat any lapse from the example set
By some exam-board. After all, how guard
Against the sheer platoons of those who'll take
Our choicest texts (or excerpts) and convert
Them into easy primers for the hard-
Of-learning, or seize every chance to make
Quite sure no passage sounds a thought-alert?

For it's going on apace in that realm too,
Let's say, the cultural-intellectual sphere
Where, as with toys or games, already we're
Unwilling witnesses as they accrue,
The handbooks, pass-notes, vain attempts to do
In short-and-simple what took many a year
Of strenuous thought before it could appear,
At some point, out of some muse-haunted blue
And thus redeem the time. I thought to head
Such *haute vulgarisation* off at source
By juxtaposing image, text and gloss
In unique constellations so they'd tread
With greater care, or take the wiser course,
Just read attentively and spurn the dross.

With toys at least there's progress of a kind,
A fast-expanding range of new techniques
In manufacture for the child who seeks
Such stimuli as benefit a mind

More techno-scientifically-inclined,
Not – as with me – the sort whose troughs and peaks
Are like those tidal moods the poet speaks
So often of, or that moon-gazers find
So much their element. No so with such
Purported gearings-up as might yet lay
My image-clusters waste, neglect the art
Of my verse-nurtured prose, and miss the touch
Of Brechtian tough-mindedness that may,
If not despoiled, give dialectics heart.

On Quotation, Shock, and Aura

> Quotations in my work are like wayside robbers who leap out armed
> and relieve the stroller of his convictions.
>
> *One Way Street and Other Writings*

Depth-charged and ready-primed, those words I quote,
A threat to all beliefs you once held dear.
Fresh powers accrue to what another wrote.

Damascus-bound when revelation smote
How shall they know what changed, at which frontier?
Depth-charged and ready-primed, those words I quote.

Sense plain enough yet might, this time, connote
Some fateful, faith-destroying new idea.
Fresh powers accrue to what another wrote.

What thought-defence against the arms they tote?
Like canny beasts of prey they sense your fear.
Depth-charged and ready-primed, those words I quote.

Best yield the point else they'll be at your throat;
Converso or Marrano: pick your steer!
Fresh powers accrue to what another wrote.

Just know: whatever set creed you devote
Your service to, the costs may be severe.
Depth-charged and ready-primed, those words I quote;
Fresh powers accrue to what another wrote.

2

> To perceive the aura of an object we look at means to invest it with
> the ability to look at us in return.
>
> 'On Some Motifs in Baudelaire'

Who's then the robber, who the passer-by?
No telling what will come of it, your stroll!
Some ricochet, however true they fly.

Return-to-sender's one trick you can try:
Quick intercept, then stroller takes control.
Who's then the robber, who the passer-by?

Such is Brecht's way: he'll listen, then reply
'Swap quotes for slogans, you unearthly soul!'.
Some ricochet, however true they fly.

The times are desperate, that I won't deny,
But those were quotes I loved and saved, not stole.
Who's then the robber, who the passer-by?

No choice citation but would signify,
To him, how marginal the scholar's role.
Some ricochet, however true they fly.

My dream: two comrades meeting eye-to-eye,
Or activist and scholar, pole-to-pole.
Who's then the robber, who the passer-by?
Some ricochet, however true they fly.

3

> [N]othing which has ever happened is to be given as lost to history.
> Indeed, the past would fully befall only a resurrected humanity.
> Said another way: only for a resurrected humanity would its past,
> in each of its moments, be citable. Each of its lived moments be-
> comes a citation *à l'ordre du jour* – whose day is precisely that of the
> Last Judgment.
>
> 'Theses on the Philosophy of History'

How stands citation to the text it cites?
No straight dependency, no one-way debt;
No source-text but's then read by tinted lights.

Call it infringement of authorial rights,
Then – try it! – state the ground-rule to be met:
How stands citation to the text it cites?

That text, once quoted, bears what it invites,
A reading apt to leave all rules upset:
No source-text but's then read by tinted lights.

I thought to write a book whose every flight's
Quote-winged, as ego-light as it could get:
Thus stands citation to the text it cites!

And yet I find there's something in me fights
For self, insists 'your life's not over yet':
No source-text but's then read by tinted lights.

Arcade-struck drifter through those lonely heights
It's I, *flâneur*, who took up Baudelaire's bet.
How stands citation to the text it cites?
No source-text but's then read by tinted lights.

4

> One might subsume the eliminated element in the term 'aura' and go
> on to say: that which withers in the age of mechanical reproduction
> is the aura of the work of art. This is a symptomatic process whose
> significance points beyond the realm of art.
>
> > 'The Work of Art in the Age of
> > Mechanical Reproduction'

It's aura yields that salutary shock,
Reminds us: all citations stake their claim.
Don't think you're drawing on some common stock.

Too much projection and you'll hit a block:
The quote will talk back, take an author-name:
It's aura yields that salutary shock.

Then you may end up in the citers' dock
Where lightly-dropped quotations bring ill fame:
Don't think you're drawing on some common stock.

There's truth in aura, truth that has us knock
Against it when we play some textual game.
It's aura yields that salutary shock.

The text looks back at us, requires we clock
Just whence, and when, and from whose hand it came:
Don't think you're drawing on some common stock.

Sometimes, indeed, it seems almost to mock
Our thought of texts as there to trade or tame.
It's aura yields that salutary shock;
Don't think you're drawing on some common stock.

5

> In the ruins of great buildings the idea of the plan speaks more im-
> pressively than in lesser buildings, however well preserved; and for
> this reason the German *Trauerspiel* merits interpretation. In the spirit
> of allegory it is conceived from the outset as a ruin, a fragment.
>
> *The Origins of German Tragic Drama*

> To great writers, finished works weigh lighter than those fragments
> on which they work throughout their lives.
>
> *One-Way Street and Other Writings*

> To read what was never written.' Such reading is the most ancient:
> reading before all languages, from the entrails, the stars, or dances.
>
> *One-Way Street and Other Writings*

How weigh them, how compute the night-hours spent
On fragments, quotes, parerga, suchlike stuff:
No finished work's their near equivalent.

They're thought's long way around to heart's content,
A state, like theirs, beyond reach, yet enough:
How weigh them, how compute the night-hours spent?

They're like those run-down quarters I frequent
Half-knowingly, or visit off-the-cuff:
No finished work's their near equivalent.

False starts and cast-offs satisfy my bent,
First drafts abandoned, street-plans sketchy, rough:
How weigh them, how compute the night-hours spent?

To read, to star-gaze so your firmament
Has chaos-zones where star-charts meet rebuff:
No finished work's their near equivalent.

They pre-empt their own ruin, circumvent
Totality, call every master's bluff.
How weigh them, how compute the night-hours spent?
No finished work's their near equivalent.

6

> Truth wants to be startled abruptly, at one stroke, from her self-im-
> mersion, whether by uproar, music, or cries for help.

One-Way Street

You scan and parse them, they return your gaze.
A steady state, but then that single stroke:
A text, a life, each yours to reappraise.

How else should reading counter the malaise
Of habitude, the pigs in custom's poke?
You scan and parse them, they return your gaze,

A placid tryst in that initial phase
But one that's apt at some point to invoke
A text, a life, each yours to reappraise.

Unsafe, those textual meadows where you'd graze
Contentedly till something made you choke.
You scan and parse them, they return your gaze,

Though suddenly a certain passage lays
On you, and you alone, the stress that woke
A text, a life, each yours to reappraise.

Like uproar, music, or distress it weighs
You on a scale from 'quit' to 'go-for-broke'.
You scan and parse them, they return your gaze;
A text, a life, each yours to reappraise.

On 'Experience'

> Because he never raises his eyes to the great and the meaningful, the philistine has taken experience as his gospel. It has become for him a message about life's commonness. But he has never grasped that there exists something other than experience, that there are values – inexperienceable – which we serve.
>
> 'Experience'

> Never has experience been more thoroughly contradicted than strategic experience was contradicted by tactical warfare, economic experience by inflation, bodily experience by mechanical warfare, moral experience by those in power.
>
> 'The Storyteller'

1

There's tales he tells and tales that stay untold.
Just ask what's shadowed forth in those he tells.
Some contradict themselves as they unfold.

It's communal, that art where he excels.
Still something holds it back, our leaning-in.
Just ask what's shadowed forth in those he tells.

Leskov, the story-teller – 'Let's begin . . . ':
Two words, and instantly the spell was cast.
Still something holds us back from leaning-in.

Call it 'experience,' that which didn't last.
They had it, shared it, let it shape their lives.
Two words and instantly the spell was cast.

Then think how story-telling lives and thrives:
No story but experience sets a seal;
They had it, shared it, let it shape their lives.

No harm should they foreknow what tales reveal:
Read fiction for those plot-twists new and bold!
No story but experience sets a seal;
There's tales he tells and tales that stay untold.

2

What's left of it, 'experience,' in our age?
At most the husks of all it once conveyed,
The proofs not far to seek or hard to gauge.

In every sphere its remnants blur and fade.
The word hangs on but owns its feeble state,
At most the husk of all it once conveyed.

Think how, in war, tacticians now dictate:
'You strategists, yield ground: we've tricks to run!'.
The word hangs on but owns its feeble state.

Then think what economic harm it's done,
Inflation off-the-scale and chaos loose:
'You strategists, yield ground: we've tricks to run!'.

And then: what moral creed of any use
Where power alone can formulate the code?
Inflation off-the-scale and chaos loose.

No room for that old story-telling mode,
No need for lessons from the local sage
Where power alone can formulate the code:
What's left of it, 'experience,' in our age?

3

Let's not get dewy-eyed about all this.
The tales he told might not be so benign;
There's bad folk, too, find cause to reminisce.

Some folksy yarns might simply fall in line
And dull thought's edge, though others make you think.
The tales he told might not be so benign.

Still some hold out as thought-horizons shrink:
There's tales resist each soothing substitute.
Some dull thought's edge, though others make you think.

Else it's not raconteurs alone left mute
But histories and whole lifetimes got by rote!
There's tales resist each soothing substitute.

Shun those who've bare life-digests to promote:
Much better trust the tale and teller too,
Not histories and whole lifetimes got by rote!

Conceive that facts alone won't come out true
If teller's warrant's something to dismiss.
Much better trust the tale and teller too
(Though not get dewy-eyed about all this).

4

'Trust to experience' – the cynic's line,
The ground of every groundless bourgeois claim
To taste or judgment by the philistine.

No thought of how 'experience' became
The refuse-bin of all thoughts gone to waste,
The ground of every groundless bourgeois claim.

The message, simply: 'count your hopes misplaced;
Experience decrees it's there they'll end,
The refuse-bin of all thoughts gone to waste'.

It's you who've got it backwards, bourgeois friend:
That bin's marked 'ideology,' not 'hope';
Experience decrees it's there they'll end.

No surer way to narrow thinking's scope:
Just fall straight back on good old common-sense!
That bin's marked 'ideology,' not 'hope'.

Truth is, you'll fill it up at thought's expense,
Lay tributes at a swindler-prophet's shrine.
Just fall straight back on good old common-sense!
'Trust to experience' – the cynic's line.

Saturnine

I came into the world under the sign of Saturn – the star of the slow-est revolution, the planet of detours and delays.

One-Way Street and Other Writings

Boredom is the dream bird that hatches the egg of experience. A rus-tling in the leaves drives him away.

'The Storyteller'

In dreams begin responsibilities.

W.B. Yeats, 'In Dreams Begin Responsibilities'

1

No true experience but begins in dreams.
Where else should fledgling judgement find its pole?
No egg to hatch save where invention teems.

It's boredom yields what dreamwork then redeems
And so gives the oneiric bird its role:
No true experience but begins in dreams.

Small hope of it from daylight thought-regimes
Where wake-up guards pass hourly on patrol.
No egg to hatch save where invention teems.

They rustle leaves, make gaps so sunlight streams,
Ensure the egg breaks neither clean nor whole:
No true experience but begins in dreams.

'*Langweiligkeit*,' most *Dichterisch* of themes;
Let 'boredom' serve for the prosaic soul!
No egg to hatch save where invention teems.

On that *langweilig* watch the one egg gleams
That time's experience-poacher never stole.
No true experience but begins in dreams;
No egg to hatch save where invention teems.

2

He eats his children, so the myths relate.
Saturnian in that – think Robespierre!
What's inwardly revolved might stay their fate.

'The slowest revolution,' one whose rate
Leaves scholars, gods and rebels time to spare.
He eats his children, so the myths relate.

The scholar's voice: consider those he ate,
How revolution's spawn may want for care.
What's inwardly revolved might stay their fate.

No *coup d'état* but bids I contemplate
What sufferings yet unrecompensed they bear.
He eats his children, so the myths relate.

My thoughts revolve as Saturn's moons rotate,
Some retrograde, so path alignments rare;
What's thus inter-involved might stay their fate.

Let activists not spurn my scholar-state,
My wandering moon that shuns the solar glare.
He eats his children, so the myths relate;
What's thus inter-involved might stay their fate.

Hashish, Aura, Revolution

Unlimited goodwill. Suspension of the compulsive anxiety complex. The beautiful 'character' unfolds. All of those present become comically iridescent. At the same time one is pervaded by their aura.

But the true, creative overcoming of religious illumination certainly does not lie in narcotics. It resides in a profane illumination, a materialistic, anthropological inspiration, to which hashish, opium, or whatever else can give an introductory lesson . . . . The reader, the thinker, the loiterer, the flâneur, are types of illuminati just as much as the opium eater, the dreamer, the ecstatic. And more profane. Not to mention that most terrible drug – ourselves – which we take in solitude.

'Protocols to the Experiments on Hashish'

1

It's scarcely 'me' at all, this selfless state.
No more the fears, neuroses, anxious tics;
No state or stage the self might calibrate.

Naught here of furtive fumbling for a fix:
It's Baudelaire, hashish-high on lyric wings.
No more the fears, neuroses, anxious tics.

What but this boundless goodwill truly brings
Such blest release from ego and its ills?
It's Baudelaire, hashish-high on lyric wings.

As ego empties so the aura fills
And holds our fragile selfhoods in suspense:
Such blest release from ego and its ills!

All beauty pleads we lower its defence,
Let good form go when beauty gently shows
It holds our fragile selfhoods in suspense.

None but the hashish-user truly knows
How ego shrinks as aura's bounds dilate.

Let good form go when beauty gently shows
It's scarcely 'me' at all, this selfless state.

2

Mere change of 'character' comes nowhere near.
I do not use but cite the word, you'll note.
Its mention brings out what's at issue here.

Change that alone, the referent of my quote,
And you'll just shuffle traits, see which might do.
I do not use but cite the word, you'll note.

When hashish hits you are no longer you.
The aura fills you, yet it's aura shared,
Else you'll just shuffle traits, see which might do.

We hashish-users end up language-snared!
Too stolid 'character,' too private 'soul'.
The aura fills you, yet it's aura shared.

Those shrewd remarks of Hegel took their toll:
What beauteous soul would gladly own the name?
Too stolid 'character,' too private 'soul'.

A thing of utmost beauty, all the same,
For souls conjoined in its auratic sphere.
What beauteous soul would gladly own the name?
Yet change of 'character' comes nowhere near.

3

My friends, they shimmer, sparkle, iridesce!
Almost it's comic, how the aura spreads
To form the perfect sphere we co-possess.

Like some great work of art, the glow it sheds.
Just now, let replication cease to thrive!
Almost it's comic, how the aura spreads.

Unique, authentic, since experienced live –

How not respond, *Kulturkritik* aside?
Just now, let replication cease to thrive!

My comrade Brecht demurs, advises I'd
Much better think 'Let copies multiply!'.
How not respond, *Kulturkritik* aside?

He says it's the hashish I'm fuddled by.
'What price that bourgeois-junkie *Innenwelt*;
Much better think "let copies multiply!"'.

Depth-analysed as well as deeply felt,
My protocols: no tripping to excess!
'What price that bourgeois-junkie *Innenwelt*?'.
My friends, they shimmer, sparkle, iridesce.

4

Conceive the perfect copy, if you can.
Bid this last fond farewell to Plato's ghost:
What if a copy framed the master-plan?

You, comrade, joke and say I've overdosed.
I say: some thoughts portend an empire's fall;
Bid this last fond farewell to Plato's ghost.

You say 'those classy multiples recall
What riles them up, the bourgeois connoisseurs'.
I say: some thoughts portend an empire's fall.

Think, then, how great the panic this one stirs:
The copyist's mark reads 'point of origin' –
That riles them up, the bourgeois connoisseurs!

Make this your version of original sin:
The boss-class lie that stole the people's art!
The copyist's mark reads 'point of origin'.

Here we might find agreement, mind and heart:
The people's activist, the one who ran

To ground the lie that stole the people's art!
Conceive the perfect copy, if you can.

5

Let striving for it be your chief reward.
No masterpiece, *chef d'oeuvre*, 'work itself'.
In its perfection see perfection flawed.

Leave those Old Masters on the boss's shelf!
He knows their price, each one, but not their worth.
No masterpiece, *chef d'oeuvre*, 'work itself'.

We Marxists bring aesthetics back to earth:
We show the lord's junk-hoard, the boss's dross;
He knows their price, each one, but not their worth.

We go our ways around, yet our paths cross
Where pain and suffering raise their age-old cry.
We show the lord's junk-hoard, the boss's dross.

Our task is revolution, you and I.
What pardon should we let that prospect go
Where pain and suffering raise their age-old cry?

Else, friend, we've nothing left to overthrow
Except all chance of working in accord.
What pardon should we let that prospect go?
Let striving for it be our chief reward.

Culture and Eros: a catechism

And we speak of the sexualisation of the spirit: this is the morality of the prostitute. She represents culture in Eros; Eros, who is the most powerful individualist, the most hostile to culture – even he can be perverted; even he can serve culture.

Letter to Herbert Belmore, June 23rd 1913.

The historical materialist leaves it to others to be drained by the whore called 'Once upon a time' in historicism's bordello.

'Theses on the Philosophy of History'

1

Reader, I beg you: do not think I write
These words as if to strike some lofty pose
Of moral rectitude, or take my place
Amongst the pious frauds who catechise

Their tabloid-reading public from the height
Of some press-baron's pulpit where what goes
Down best is what equates your state of grace
With showing you're one of those regular guys

Who loves home-life, takes Jesus as his light
(One query: Mary Magdalen?), and knows
One thing for sure: that there's a master-race
Those whores had better greet with open thighs!

I'd meet you honestly on this: alright,
I've paid for sex, enjoyed what she bestows,
That 'fallen woman,' thrilled to her embrace,
And not, like them, affected to despise

The sensuous pleasure of a wondrous night
When each accepts what the encounter owes
To chance, need, deprivation, or – worst case –
The lack of everything that money buys

Of creature-sustenance and so holds tight,
As creature-kind, to him or her who shows
A loving-back no payment can debase
Since freed of all those life-degrading lies!

Believe me, then, as one who's known the blight
Of loneliness in exile, and who chose
To populate that unfrequented space
With a transaction nothing could disguise –

No bourgeois show of marriage-troths to plight! –
Yet in whose course the simulated throes
Of ecstasy might briefly bear a trace
Of what the sex-trade failed to merchandise.

2

Or so I once convinced myself – still do,
From time to time, when exile, boredom, fear,
Or clerkly travails bring on the desire
For all that Eros offers in the way

Of comfort, intimacy, and – should you
Strike lucky – somebody who'll lend an ear
To secret griefs and so prove worth the hire,
Not merely in the sense 'a decent lay

With pillow-chat thrown in' but someone, too,
Who's doubtless travelled close to that frontier
Where vice and crime, like gun-towers and barbed wire,
Have naught but hopes extinguished to convey.

You're right – it's every punter's lenient view
Of his recurrent lapses, that idea
That each new sex-transaction might acquire
Some self-redemptive power, some brief *entrée*

To realms safe-cordoned by whatever drew
Two souls together, like the sundered sphere
Of Plato's image whose split halves aspire
To naught but their long-dreamt reunion day.

That's self-deluding stuff, I always knew,
Or half-knew – stuff concocted just to clear
The queasy conscience when it's under fire
And out of high-toned, stupid things to say.

Worse still, sex-workers yield the tribute due
From eros to the anerotic sphere
Of culture where the skimpy night-attire,
Lewd gestures, and pimp-choreographed display

Of *outré* postures herald the debut
In spirit's realm of all the kinky gear
That goes to reassure the nervous buyer
There's special stuff for those prepared to pay.

3

Twice damned – for thinking somehow to placate
My guilty soul by that tear-jerker's tale
Of the good-hearted prostitute and my
Brief spell of comfort in her arms; and more

Acutely shameful yet, the bourgeois trait
Par excellence of grand ideas that fail
As soon as tested, like the way that I,
A Marxist culture-critic, could ignore

The ideologemes that saturate
My discourse, from the crassest kind of male
Ingratiating ruse ('please let me cry
On your soft shoulder') to the sexist lore

That has each guilty punter sublimate
The object of his lust into a frail
And sympathetic listener for the guy
Who comes with psyche primed: Madonna-whore.

It's culture, bourgeois culture, and the freight
Of sexual hang-ups following in its tail
That leaves most men unable to get by
Without some psychic levelling of the score.

But how should I, long schooled to cultivate
A sense of how the sex-drive may derail
The keenest intellect, think to deny
The thought that some rogue male *esprit de corps*

Has once more had me rise to the old bait
Of that lone scholar's solace, love for sale,
That, in his working hours, he'd classify
As top-shelf items in the bourgeois store

Of eros-substitutes? They'll not dictate
My fantasies, I tell myself, or nail
My errant mind to sex-drives that belie
Its still intact capacity to draw

The requisite self-knowledge from this state,
This inner turmoil, where the conscience-flail
Gives each judge-penitent good cause to try
Himself, like Josef K before the law.

A Thought of Emma Goldman

> Life is in fact mortal, and the immortal things are flesh, energy, individuality, and spirit in its various guises.
>
> *Reflections*

> If I can't dance, I don't want to be in your revolution.
>
> Emma Goldman

Things mortal wither, perish,
Though cherish them you may;
Those thoughts of death won't vanish,
Though banished for a day,
But soon make way
For portents more nightmarish.

Mere life brings naught to hope for –
No scope for what they crave,
Those sleuths of the eternal
Who spurn all things that gave
Life savour save
Life-dues they got old rope for.

It's fleshly joy sustains us;
What pains us is to make
'Life,' that death-bound nostrum,
Our rostrum for the sake
Of creeds that take
Away what joy remains us.

It's spirit, too, that shifts us,
Gifts us truth-questing ones,
Unresting ones, admittance –
Soul's quittance! – to what shuns
Bare life and runs
Where spirit's call uplifts us.

Its energy enhances
Life-chances, yet adds: Don't now

Allow these times to break it
Or fake it, Emma's vow –
'No end to how
My revolution dances!'.

Page-Turner

Like a clock of life on which the seconds race, the page number hangs over the characters in a novel. Where is the reader who has not once lifted to it a fleeting, fearful glance?

One-Way Street and Other Writings

1

What dread is this each time you turn a page?
Speed up, slow down, their lives are theirs to lead:
No way your pace will change how fast they age.

Still there's that feeling grips you as you read,
Though good sense says 'just choose your own best pace:
Speed up, slow down, their lives are theirs to lead'.

Yet how ignore it as you start to race?
No recompense for those with lives cut short,
Though good sense says 'just choose your own best pace'.

It's Anna, Emma, Ivan Ilyich, brought
To death's door by a looming short-loan date.
No recompense for those with lives cut short.

And yet, why blame me for this vexing trait
When tragic heroes end up reader-sped
To death's door by a looming short-loan date?

For it's the old desire to see them dead,
The old generic drive that has its way
When tragic heroes end up reader-sped.

Let's face it: readers get the final say,
Presage the obits, set the fifth-act stage,
The old generic drive that has its way:
What dread is this each time you turn a page?

2

They're doubts no easy answer can assuage.
Must others pay as readers up the speed?
The cost for them – impossible to gauge!

It's ours, the life from time's compulsion freed
And theirs, as life runs out, this truth to face:
Must others pay as readers up the speed?

Our *Lebensraum* is their lost living-space,
Their ampler life-time what our needs abort
And theirs, as life runs out, that truth to face.

'Strong readers rule,' the latest trends report.
From year to year we reel in others' fate;
Their ampler life-time's what our needs abort.

With fictive lives and real we fix the date:
Things done, undone, pre-empted, left unsaid.
From year to year we reel in others' fate.

There's some who'll gaily cut the vital thread;
Why fret if leaps wipe years off as they may,
Things done, undone, pre-empted, left unsaid?

Myself, I think there's penalties to pay,
Uncertainties to plague the placid sage.
Why fret if leaps wipe years off as they may?
They're doubts no easy answer can assuage.

Anabasis: Port Bou

You admit that for the time being you do not want to accept commu-
nism 'as the solution for humanity'. But of course the issue is precisely
to abolish the unproductive pretensions of solutions for humanity
by means of the feasible findings of this very system; indeed, to give
up entirely the immodest prospect of 'total' systems and at least to
make the attempt to construct the days of humanity in just as loose a
fashion as a rational person who has had a good night's sleep begins
his day.

Bertolt Brecht, Letter to Benjamin, April 1936

Every line we succeed in publishing today – no matter how uncertain
the future to which we entrust it – is a victory wrenched from the
powers of darkness.

Benjamin, Letter to Gershom Scholem, January 1940

And shall I then have come so far to find
My life as wandering scholar brought to book
By exile, war, and character combined,
Along with what I once, naively, took
As my appointed task on earth: to find
In textual labyrinths what I forsook
In action, or to deem the pensive mind
Fit place, in these thrice-dreadful times, to look
For hope renewed? I have them here, my last,
Most urgent yet, as always, cryptic notes
From this, as always, melancholy phase
Of my now vagrant life, frail missives cast
On waters where the only stuff that floats
Is stuff best suited to these end-time days.

My 'Theses on Philosophy of . . . ' – what?
Well, 'History,' the title runs – eighteen
Reflections on such topics as you'll not,
Perhaps, count relevant but may just glean
An inkling of should something hit the spot,
As when the Angel's *Rücksicht* brings a scene
Like our *Blitzkrieg* to come, or how we've got

Just this last chance to interdict what's been
And make good what's to come. But then the thought
Recurs with doubled force: you, Benjamin:
What words are these from one who always turned
To books, not actions, and who never brought
His reading to the point of issuing in
The Brechtian praxis he admired yet spurned?

Now on this lethal border still I strive
To think they did some good, the texts, the flights
Of speculative commentary that I've
So occupied my life with, days and nights,
That they alone made me feel man alive,
Left me convinced that picking daily fights
With Nazi hoodlums merely boosts the drive
To violence, death, and all the appetites
That flock to Hitler's call. Yet well I know
(And had Bert to remind me): leave aside
The pedagogy, calls to action, street-
Assemblies, posters, hand-outs, times to show
Off our collective muscle, and we'll slide
Back into one more open-goal defeat.

They're with me in this suit-case, the last fruits
Of a life's-work foreshortened by the fate
That's led me here – albeit in cahoots
With my own disposition – to this state
Of statelessness, this end to all the routes
I've travelled, routes oblique yet heading straight,
As if by border-striding seven-league boots,
To Port Bou and the fifth-act poisoned bait
That marks me Hamlet's kin. Those Theses may
Survive, find readers, even – if I dare
Stretch hope so far – some readers well-equipped
To parse them with due notice of the way
I write with one eye to the world out there
And one to some redemptive future-script.

This strange binocularity has lost
Me comrades, friends, 'connections,' any lift
Of academic fortunes, and – the cost
Most grievous – what so suffered in that rift
With Brecht when our two lives were exile-tossed
And everything conspired to have us drift
Our separate ways, I to old writings glossed
In quest of unknown truths, he with his gift
For play-texts bang on theme. No choice, I fear:
My *vita ante acta*'s come to this
Near-Oedipal last stage where poison-pill's
My one choice that avoids the non-frontier
Between two lands, two different ways to miss
What might yet have redeemed the life it kills.

About the Author

Chris Norris is Emeritus Professor in Philosophy at the University of Cardiff. He is the author or editor of more than forty academic books on aspects of philosophy, literature, the history of ideas, politics, and music. Among his chief interests are the poetry and criticism of William Empson and the writings of Jacques Derrida and Alain Badiou.

He has also published a number of poetry collections: *The Cardinal's Dog*; *For the Tempus-Fugitives*; *The Matter of Rhyme*; *A Partial Truth*; *As Knowing Goes*; *Hedgehogs: Verse Reflections after Derrida*; *Damaged Life: Poems after Adorno's Minima Moralia*; *Socrates at Verse*; *Recalibrating and Other Poems*; *After Rilke: Renderings, Parodies, Rejoinders and Animadversions*; and *A Listener and Other Poems about Music*. His political verse has appeared in three volumes: *The Trouble with Monsters, The Folded Lie, and Convulsions, 2021–2024: A Trusstercluck*.

He has lectured, given poetry-readings, and held visiting posts at numerous universities in countries including the UK, the US, China, Canada, India, Spain, South Korea, Japan, Germany, South Africa, Morocco, Switzerland, Egypt, Serbia, Ireland, and Fiji. A previous verse-collection of his was a Times Literary Supplement "Book of the Year" (Terry Eagleton's choice) and he has now become very much involved in the innovative field of Creative Criticism.

Photograph of the author by
Valerie Norris. Used by permission.

9 781643 175102